THE
LIVERPOOL & LONDON
AND GLOBE
INSURANCE COMPANY.

FIRE AND LIFE.

Directors in Canada:
HON. HENRY STARNES, Chairman.
EDMOND J. BARBEAU, ESQ., Deputy-Chairman.
WENTWORTH J. BUCHANAN, ESQ.
ANDREW FREDERICK GAULT, ESQ.
SAMUEL FINLEY, ESQ.

AVAILABLE ASSETS	$46,872,992
BALANCE OF SUBSCRIBED CAPITAL NOT CALLED UP	8,771,800
TOTAL,	**$55,644,792**

In addition to which we have the unlimited liability of wealthy shareholders.

PARTICULARS OF ASSETS:

Capital Paid up	$1,228,200
General Reserve	6,500,000
Fire Re-Insurance	3,700,000
Balance Profit and Loss	4,145,597
Globe Perpetual Fund	5,514,000
Life and Annuity Fund	23,042,387
Other Funds as Enumerated in Balance Sheet	2,742,808
	$46,872,992

THE INCOME IN 1894 WAS FOR

Fire Premiums, after deducting Re-Insurances	$8,090,640
Life Premiums, do. do. do.	1,161,740
Interest derived from Investments	1,726,526
Annual Income	**$10,978,906**
Or, say average Daily Income of	**$30,079**
Total Claims Paid by the Company since its commencement	$157,878,457

Insurances Effected at the Lowest Current Rates.

Head Office, Canada Branch: MONTREAL.

G. F. C. SMITH,
Chief Agent and Resident Secretary.

The patronage of the Insuring Public is solicited.

THE LATE WALTER H. SMITH.

SMITH'S
PLANETARY ALMANAC
AND
WEATHER GUIDE.

1896   1896

A PLANETARY EPHEMERIS CALCULATED TO MONTREAL MEAN TIME ;
THE STARS IN THEIR SEASONS ;

LUNAR INFLUENCE ON VEGETATION,

WITH TABLES FOR SOWING ACCORDING TO IT IN ALL LATITUDES; A LIST OF
MOONLIGHT EVENINGS; COPIOUS ASTRONOMICAL AND
METEOROLOGICAL NOTES, ETC.

BY THE LATE

WALTER H. SMITH.

A LIFE OF THE LATE WALTER H. SMITH: A GENERAL FORECAST FOR THE
YEAR; AN OUTLINE SKETCH OF THE WEATHER BY MONTHS; THE

WEATHER FOR EACH WEEK,

BY

JAMES H. OXLEY.

MONTREAL:
215 PINE AVENUE.
1895.

LIFE OF WALTER H. SMITH,

Astronomer and Meteorologist.

By J. H. Oxley.

THE writer became acquainted with the late Mr. Smith in the year 1874, in the office of the *Montreal Daily Witness*. Having just left school, and being in that transition state between boyhood and manhood, I have always considered myself peculiarly fortunate in finding such a companion at that period ; and the acquaintance thus formed speedily ripened into warm friendship, owing to a similarity of literary tastes.

From his earliest youth Mr. Smith had been delicate, with a sensitive, retiring disposition, but endowed with an energy and capacity for diverse mental studies which astonished his more intimate friends. His evenings were spent in company with the writer for many years, and were characterised by a greater amount of application and a higher range of study than the majority of young men indulge in. At this period my friend enjoyed fairly good health, and having a mind well-stored with information, and with good conversational powers, he proved a delightful companion. He was one of those who, like Bryant, loved to " enter the wild wood and view the haunts of nature," and in the early spring mornings would wend his way to Mount Royal while its spring dress was yet in embyro. It was during these rambles that the writer learned to love his companion, and to note the general bias of his mind. The subtle charm of poesy seems to have pervaded him, and this spell of fancy and feeling, of imagination and truth, was brought to the surface by trifles. He would be enthusiastic over the discovery of a violet " half-hidden in a mossy dell," and search for them among the decayed leaves and *debris* of the winter as eagerly

MURRAY, BALL & CO.,

Dealers in Mantles and Fireplaces, Tile Work

OF ALL DESCRIPTIONS,

40 BLEURY STREET, MONTREAL.

We are new beginners, therefore we wish to bring ourselves before you. When we say new beginners, we do not mean inexperienced, but merely to say we have started in business. We have had fifteen years' experience with the largest firms here as practical workmen, and we are now prepared to carry out any contract in this line in a first-class manner. Our aim is to lead with the style, quality and latest patterns of the century. We employ none but the best workmen in order to give satisfaction to everyone. We also carry in stock fireplace furnishings, and make a specialty of supplying fine marble tiling, bathrooms, floors, counters, and windows, and laying mosaic pavements. We will be pleased to have you give us a call, and will guarantee good substantial work and satisfaction at moderate charges.

ARCHITECTS' DESIGNS FAITHFULLY CARRIED OUT.

T. E. & A. MARTIN,

Have a good assortment of ARM

From $3.00 and upwards.

1924 NOTRE DAME STREET,

MONTREAL.

as would a child. Though of a gentle, affectionate, and somewhat timid disposition, he was withal very tenacious of his
opinions, and was ever ready to do battle in defence of his
views, and did not take too kindly to opposition in any form.
As a young man he was hungry and thirsty for knowledge,
influence and fame ; and it was quite natural, with his heart
full of hope and his brain full of ambition, that he was eager
his name should be frequently found among communications
to the press, and not surprising that while still young he
soon attracted the notice of scientists, who eventually paved
the way to what proved to be his pet science and life work—
astronomy and weather forecasting. With these few words
of personal tribute, I give below a more extended notice of
Mr. Smith's life.

Mr Smith was born at Canonbury, London, England, on
September 12th., 1852. He was the youngest son of a
family descended from three famous races, namely, King
Alfred's West Saxons, the Covenanters of Scotland, and the
Huguenots of France. Owing to sickness, his routine educa-
tion ended at 12 years of age (1864), after which the world
became his school. Between 12 and 21 he devoured every
scrap of knowledge that fell in his way. He thus learned
many things, including astronomy, meteorology, occultism,
rhyme, modelling in clay, illuminating, freehand drawing
and entomology. At thirteen he was an adept at modelling,
obtaining "honorable mention" at the Metropolitan and
Provincial Industrial Exhibition, held in the Agricultural
Hall, London, in competition against all comers. Later, he
took prizes for freehand drawing, antique lettering and pen
and ink drawing in England and Canada, his "Genealogy of
Princess Louise" and "Voyage of Jacques Cartier" at the
Dominion Exhibition of 1880 having drawn the attention of
H. R. H. the Princess Louise and His Excellency Lord
Lorne. He made an exhaustive collection of Canadian and
British Diurnal Lepidoptera (butterflies), and was for some
years a member of the Entomological Society of Ontario.
Beginning to write verse in England during the agitation for
and the passage of the "Representation of the People" bill
(1867-8), he took the popular side with Gladstone and Bright,
and remained steadfast to the Liberal cause both in England
and Canada. He was also a Prohibitionist.

Upon reaching Montreal, in 1874, he shortly after entered the *Daily Witness* office, and was a member of its local staff till his final illness, which resulted in his death, May 3rd. A great number of his contributions to science and poetry made their first appearance in the *Witness*. His scientific contributions introduced him to the late Mr. H. G. Vennor, F.G.S., the Canadian weather prophet, who induced Mr. Smith (1882) to become astronomical editor of *Vennor's Almanac, Vennor's Weather Bulletin*, etc. After the death of Mr. Vennor, in 1884, Mr. Smith continued the yearly publication under the title of SMITH'S PLANETARY ALMANAC, which he issued each year since. Its forecasts became noted. In 1884 he reported at Montreal the meetings of section 'A' (astronomy) of the British Association for the Advancement of Science. These meetings suggested to him the idea of forming an association for the study of planetary meteorology, which he accordingly did in the fall of that year at Montreal. He was elected and re-elected president while the association existed, publishing as an accessory a monthly *Astronomy and Meteorology*. In 1889, for lack of time, Mr. Smith felt obliged to withdraw from the association, since which time it ceased to meet. At its most prosperous period (1887) the Astro-Meteorological Association met regularly at Montreal, besides having branches in several of the United States. Since 1882, when he began to contribute scientific articles to the Canadian press, his communications on astronomy, meteorology and planetary influence numbered several hundreds. They appeared in various publications. In 1882, it is said, he was the first in Canada to point a telescope at the Crul's comet; in 1888 he passed several months of nightly study of the belts and spots on Jupiter. In 1889 he devoted several months to the rectification and "re-discovery" of the markings on Venus, and was for some years one of the first to observe and report coincident appearances of sun-spots and aurora. A writer of unique poems on astronomical subjects, he was also an able lecturer in fields connected with his pet science. Mr. Smith married, in 1878, Mary Elizabeth, daughter of Mr. James Lawrence, of Little Marlow, England.

NINETEENTH ANNUAL ADDRESS.

 JUST as the late Mr. Smith had completed the astronomical part of the 1896 issue of SMITH'S PLANETARY ALMANAC, he was taken suddenly ill, and passed away on the 3rd May, leaving the weather predictions, together with other miscellaneous astronomical calculations, still untouched. My friend had for years known that his heart was affected, but had suffered no serious inconvenience from it up to September 4th., 1894, when he was taken ill on the street, and a few days later (Sept. 6th) determined to take a brief respite from journalistic worries. From this time he remained quietly resting at home, sick, but not incapacitated for literary labour until the early days of April, 1895, when the conviction was forced upon him that his heart was slowly but surely failing, and on the 21st inst. he took to bed, from which he was destined never to rise.

That he had some hopes of final recovery, or at least a condition which, though far enough removed from the terra firma of established health, would enable him to still follow his favourite studies, is evinced by the following lines, written a short time after the weather forecast for 1895 had been finished :

"Why, only a few weeks since, it looked as if my final forecast had been written. Returned from an approach to the 'Valley of the Shadow,' it is meet and pleasant, in these quiet days of convalesence to take up my pen. No need for me to regret the lapse of those balmy September days, or to note with dismay that blustery October is here, with its sodden fields and its wind-swept denuded trees, with their

> "One red leaf, the last of its clan,
> That dances as often as dance it can,
> Hanging so light, and hanging so high,
> On the topmost twig that looks up at the sky."

"For am I not as one who has taken a new lease of life?"

But his lease of life was brief, and a short time after his burial, Mrs. Smith proposed that I should continue the

Almanac. Though familiar with Mr. Smith's methods of weather forecasting, it was with great diffidence that I entered on the work. The probabilities given week by week, and the forecasts by month, are therefore calculated by myself, and are the result of careful computations on the Astro-Meteorological system, which proved so successful in the hands of the late Mr. Smith.

If the probabilities be found at variance with the actual weather, I beg the public to believe that the fault is in me, and not in the system. Astro-Meteorology, or the planetary positions for every day in the year, is the general basis on which the forecasts in this work are built. Though for many years familiar with the basis of the system, and in close touch with Mr. Smith since his arrival in Canada, I may misinterpret at times; but the broad facts are ever patent to the careful observer, that it is the exponent of the system who is in error, and not the system itself. Those who are inclined to think that weather forecasting is pure guess-work, will doubtless be surprised to learn that my probabilities for 1896 were in the hands of the printer on the first of August, 1895. Let those of my readers who are sceptical of the lines on which I work try their skill at fore-casting for, say, a month in advance. The chances are that after a trial they will be more indulgent to errors on the part of those who are working out the weather problem on scientific grounds.

In conclusion, I repeat that though I may make mistakes at the outset, the success of the system in the past encourages me to proceed, and because I feel that the weather is a subject of vast import to toiling millions on this Continent, and worthy the most studious attention of thoughtful minds, and should the forecasts prove fairly successful this year, I hope to continue them next.

JAMES H. OXLEY.

MONTREAL,
Octob:r 7th, 1895.

ASTRONOMICAL AND OTHER NOTES.

[The calculations in this Almanac are in " Montreal Mean Time," which is 5 min. 43 sec. fast of " Eastern Standard Time."]

FIXED AND MOVABLE FESTIVALS, 1896.

Being Bissextile, or Leap Year, and the 59th-60th of Queen Victoria's Reign, as well as the latter part of the 29th, and the beginning of the 30th year of the Confederation composing the Provinces of the Dominion of Canada.

New Year's Day—} Circumcision. }	....Jan.	1	Trinity Sunday.........	"	31
Epiphany, Russian } New Year.... }	"	6	Birth of Duke of } York, 1865..... }	June	3
Septuagesima Sunday...Feb.		2	Corpus Christi...	"	4
Quinquagesima— } Shrove Sunday. }	"	16	Accession of Queen } Victoria, 1837.... }	"	20
Ash Wednesday........	"	19	St. John Baptist, } Midsummer day.. }	"	24
Washington's Birthday..	"	22	Coronation of Queen } Victoria, 1838..... }	"	28
First Sunday in Lent...	"	23	St. Peter and St. Paul...	"	29
St. David ....Mar.		1	Dominion Day.........July		1
Mid Lent Sunday.	"	15	Independence Day	"	4
St. Patrick............	"	17	Labor Day (Monday)...Sept.		7
Annunciation—Lady Day	"	25	Michaelmas.	"	29
Palm Sunday	"	29	Hallowe'en ....Oct.		31
Maunday Thursday....Apr.		2	All Saints Day........ .Nov.		1
Good Friday	"	3	Birth of Prince of } Wales, 1841.... }	"	9
Easter Sunday !........	"	5	Advent Sunday.........	"	29
Low Sunday	"	12	St. Andrew.........	"	30
St. George	"	23	Birth of Princess of } Wales, 1844..... }	Dec.	1
Rogation Sunday.......May		10	Conception B. V. M.....	"	8
Ascension Day— } Holy Thursday. }	"	14	St. Thomas.....	"	21
Birth of Queen } Victoria, 1819. }	"	24	Christmas Day (Friday).	"	25
Pentecost—Whit-Sunday	"	24			

PRINCIPAL ARTICLES OF THE CALENDAR.

Lunar Cycle or Golden Number	16	Dominical Letter	E.D.
Epact...........	15	Roman Indiction	9
Solar Cycle:.....	1	Julian Period	.6609

BUSINESS HOLIDAYS.
Canada.

QUEBEC—New Year's Day (Jan. 1st); Epiphany (Jan. 6th); Good Friday (April 3rd); Easter Monday (April 6th); Ascension day (May 14th); Queen's Birthday (May 24th); Dominion Day (July 1st); Labor Day (Sept. 7th); All Saints (Nov. 1st); Conception (Dec. 8th), and Christmas Day (Dec. 25th)

, ONTARIO and the rest of the DOMINION—New Year's Day, Ash Wednesday (Feb. 19th), Good Friday, Easter Monday, Queen's Birthday and Christmas Day.

Also, throughout the Dominion, any day appointed by Proclamation a Public Feast or Thanksgiving Day.

United States.

New Year's Day, Washington's Birthday (Feb. 22nd), Decoration Day (May 30th), Independence Day (July 4th), Labor Day, Election Day (Nov. 3rd), Thanksgiving Day (Nov. 26th) and Christmas Day.

MASSACHUSETTS also celebrates Bunker Hill Day (June 17th), and CALIFORNIA, Admission Day (Sept. 9th).

England and Ireland.

Good Friday, Easter Monday, Whit Monday (May 25th), First Monday in August, Christmas Day and Boxing Day (Dec 26th)

Scotland.

New Year's Day, Good Friday, First Monday in May, First Monday in August and Christmas Day.

France.

New Year's Day, Easter Monday, Ascension Day, Whit Monday, National Holiday (July 14th), All Saints Day, Christmas Day and Boxing Day.

CHRONOLOGICAL ERAS.

The first day of January of the year 1896 is the 2,413,-560th day since the commencement of, and the 6609th year of the Julian Period.

The year 1896 is the 7404–7405 of the Byzantine Era, the year 7405 commencing on September 1st.

The year 5656–57 of the Jewish Era, the year 5657 commencing on September 8th, or more exactly at sunset on September 7th.

The year 2649 since the foundation of Rome, according to VARRO.

The year 2643 since the beginning of the Era of NABON-ASSAR, which has been assigned to Wednesday, the 26th of February of the 3967th year of the Julian Period; corresponding, in the notation of chronologists, to the 747th; and in the notation of astronomers, to the 746th year before the birth of CHRIST.

The year 2672 of the Olympiads, or the fourth year of the 668th Olympiad, commencing in July, 1896, if we fix the Era of the Olympiads at 775½ years before Christ, or near the beginning of July of the year 3938 of the Julian Period.

The year 2208 of the Grecian Era, or the Era of the Seleucidæ.

The year 1612 of the Era of Diocletian, and the year 2556 of the Japanese Era.

The year 1314 of the Mohammedan Era, or the Era of the Hegira, commences on June 12th, 1896.

The 121st year of the Independence of the United States of America begins on July 4th, 1896.

The 30th year of the Confederation of the Provinces of the Dominion of Canada begins on July 1st, 1896.

The year 1896 is the 404th–5th since the discovery of America by Columbus, October 12th, 1492.

The 288th–9th since the foundation of Quebec by Champlain in 1608.

The 254th–5th since the foundation of Montreal by Maisonneuve on May 17th, 1642.

The 130th–31st since the Treaty which confirmed the possession of Canada to the British in 1766.

COMMENCEMENT OF THE SEASONS.

Montreal Mean Time.

The Sun enters ♈ (0° Longitude) and SPRING begins March 19th, at 9h. evening.

The Sun enters ♋ (90° Longitude) and SUMMER begins June 20th, at 5h. evening.

The Sun enters ♎ (180° Longitude) and AUTUMN begins September 22nd, at 8h. morning.

The Sun enters ♑ (270° Longitude) and WINTER begins December 21st, at 2h. morning.

The EQUINOXES happen when Spring and Autumn begin, and the SOLSTICES at the Commencement of Summer and Winter.

The Earth is in PERIHELION—nearest the Sun and distant from it 91,300,000 miles—at 1h. evening, on January 1st, 1896, and in APHELION—farthest from the Sun and distant from it 94,300,000 miles—at 5h. evening, on July 3rd, 1896.

SIGNS OF THE ZODIAC.

These are twelve, and given for mean moon at Montreal, in "the Moon" column of each calendar page. They are as follows : ♈ Aries (Head and Face), the Ram ; ♉ Taurus (Neck), the Bull ; ♊ Gemini (Arms and Shoulders), the Twins ; ♋ Cancer (Breast), the Crab ; ♌ Leo (Heart), the Lion ; ♍ Virgo (Bowels), the Virgin ; ♎ Libra (Kidneys and Back), the Balance ; ♏ Scorpio (Secrets), the Scorpion ; ♐ Sagittarius (Thighs), the Archer ; ♑ Capricornus (Knees), the Goat ; ♒ Aquarius (Legs), the Water Bearer ; and ♓ Pisces (Feet), the Fishes.

ASTRONOMICAL SYMBOLS.

PLANETS.—☉ Sun, ☿ Mercury, ♀ Venus, ⊕ Earth, ☾ Moon, ♂ Mars, ♃ Jupiter, ♄ Saturn, ♅ Uranus, ♆ Neptune.

ECLIPSES.

In the year 1896 there will be four eclipses, two of the Sun (☉) and two of the Moon (☾).

1.—An Annular Eclipse of the Sun (☉), February 13th, invisible at Montreal. Visible over the South Atlantic Ocean, Cape Colony, Cape Horn, the Falkland Islands, and Antarctic Ocean. Montreal mean time of the Conjunction in Right Ascension, 10h. 38m. 08s. morn.

2.—A Partial Eclipse of the Moon (☾), February 28th, invisible at Montreal. Visible in Europe, Asia, and Africa. Montreal mean time of the Opposition in Right Ascension, 2h. 51m. 31s. eve. Magnitude of the Eclipse., = 0.871 (Moon's diameter, = 1,000).

3.—A Total Eclipse of the Sun (☉), August 8th, invisible at Montreal. Visible over Alaska, Siberia, Japan, China, Russia, Norway, Sweden, etc. Montreal mean time of the Conjunction in Right Ascension, 11h. 43m. 02s. eve.

4.—A Partial Eclipse of the Moon (☾), August 22nd-23rd, visible at Montreal. The beginning visible over western Europe, the Atlantic Ocean, North and South America, and the Pacific Ocean. Moon enters penumbra, Montreal mean time, 11h. 14m. eve ; enters shadow (beginning of eclipse), 0h. 20m. morn.; middle of eclipse, 2h. 03m. morn ; leaves shadow (end of eclipse), 3h. 36m. morn.; leaves penumbra, 4h. 52m. morn. Magnitude of the eclipse, = 0.734 (Moon's diameter, = 1).

MERCURY (☿) 1896.

This Planet should be looked for as "Morning Star," when elongated west of the Sun, and as "Evening Star," when elongated east of the Sun, as follows:

"MORNING STAR."			"EVENING STAR."		
Mar. 5, Elongated West,	27° 20'	Jan. 24, Elongated East,	18° 31'
July 3, ,, ,,	21° 25'	May 16, ,, ,,	22° 09'
Oct. 24, ,, ,,	18° 26'	Sept. 13 ,, ,,	26° 43'

Venus, March 3rd, 1889, at 6h. 50m. Montreal time. Drawn by W. H. Smith.

VENUS (♀) 1896.

Venus, at the entry of 1896, is near the Sun in the Morning Sky. She reaches Superior Conjunction (beyond the Sun) on July 9th, when she becomes an "Evening Star" for the rest of the year.

[For descriptive illustrated article, see "views of Venus," in SMITH's PLANETARY ALMANAC for 1890, price 12 cents, post paid.]

MOONLIGHT EVENINGS OF 1896.

January.—From the 22nd to the 30th.

February.—From the 21st to the 29th.

March—Between the 22nd and the 30th.

April.—Beginning on the 20th and lasting until the 28th.

May.—From the 20th until the 27th.

June.—Beginning on the 18th and lasting until the 26th.

July.—From the 17th until the 26th.

August.—Beginning on the 15th and lasting until the 24th.

September.—From the 13th until the 24th.

October.—Beginning on the 13th and continuing until the 23rd.

November.—From the 12th until the 21st.

December.—Beginning on the 11th and lasting until the 21st.

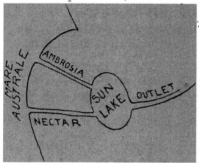

Lake of the Sun, with inlets and outlets.
Martian Latitude South 19° to 32°.

MARS (♂) 1896.

The "Fiery Planet" will prove very interesting in 1896, reaching Opposition (brightest) on December 10th-11th, at midnight. Observers with even small telescopes may expect to see some of the wonders upon his disc, provided they know where to look for them. Drawings of the "Lake of the Sun" and the "South Polar Ice Cap" of

Mars.—South Polar Ice Cap.—1894.

Mars as they appeared during the Opposition of 1894, will no doubt prove of interest. Mars will be a "Morning Star" from January 1st to December 10th, 1896, and an "Evening Star" for the rest of the year. His apparent disc will vary from 0.852 in August, to 1.000 in December. The periodic times of the Satellites are:

Satellites	Time of Revolution.
PHOBOS (I)	0d. 7h. 39m. 14s.
DEIMOS (II)	1d. 6h. 17m. 54s.

[For descriptive illustrated article, see "Markings on Mars," in SMITH'S PLANETARY ALMANAC for 1892, price 12 cents, post-paid]

THE ASTEROIDS, 1896.

These small bodies now number over 400. The greater part are, however, exceedingly small, and practically without interest to the amateur Astronomer.

CERES (1)—with a linear diameter, according to the Lick observations, of 599 miles—reaches Opposition—brightest, is overhead at midnight, and best placed for telescopic observation on September 21st, 1896. Her Right Ascension is then 0h. 24m. 11s. Declination South, 14° 37′ 38.″ A spot in the Constellation *Cetus*, about 3° North of *Beta* (*Diphda*).

PALLAS (2) is at Opposition, August 16th, 1896. Its R. A. is then 21h. 13m. 45s.; Declination N. 10° 50' 51". A spot in the Constellation *Pegasus*, on the border of *Equuleus.*

JUNO (3) reaches Opposition on December 17th, 1896. Her R. A. is then 5h. 47m. 55s. ; Declination S. 0° 57' 31". A spot in the Constellation *Orion*, a little East of the three stars in the belt.

VESTA (4) is at Opposition on December 21st, 1896. Her R.A. is then 6h. 2m. 39s, ; Declination N. 20° 51' 23". A spot in the upper portion of the Constellation *Orion*, on the border of *Gemini.*

MONTREAL MEAN TIME.

ON MERIDIAN (SOUTH).	July 15th.	Aug. 20th.	Sept. 13th.	Oct. 6th.
Ceres	5 08 mo.	2 49 mo.	1 01 mo.	11 07 ev.
Pallas.........	2 03 mo.	11 18 ev.	9 25 ev.	7 48 ev.

	Oct. 7th.	Nov. 12th.	Dec. 17th.	Jan. 10th, 1897.
Juno..........	4 46 mo.	2 43 mo.	11 59 ev.	10 08 ev.
Vesta.........	5 20 mo.	3 08 mo.	0 20 mo.	10 19 ev.

JUPITER'S ($\mathrm{2\!\!\!/}$) SATELLITES, 1896.

Some additional facts of interest respecting the new Satellite of Barnard (V) have become public since my issue of last year. Its mean distance from the centre of Jupiter is found to be 112,000 miles, or about 67,000 from the Primary's surface. Its orbit is quite elliptic, while the orbits of the other four are almost round. Its motion amounts to over $16\frac{1}{4}$ miles per second ; which makes it the most rapid satellite known. More rapid by twelve times than the motion of Phobos, the inner satellite of Mars. It is computed to be about 100 miles in diameter. Several names, including " Columbia," " Eureka " and " Amalthea " have been suggested, but its discoverer says that he prefers it to remain as at first called viz : " The fifth satellite."

The four larger Satellites are visible in small telescopes from January 1st to July 13th, and from September 10th to the end of the year. The fifth Satellite has thus far only been seen in the following giant lenses :—Mr. Common's 5 foot mirror (England) ; Lick Observatory, 36 inch refractor ;

Naval Observatory, Washington, 26 inch; University of Virginia, 26 inch; Cambridge University (England), 25 inch; Princeton University, 23 inch; and Evanston (Ill.), 18½ inch.

The Satellite's mean Synodic periods, or times of revolution:

Satellites.	Time of Revolution.
BARNARD'S (V)	0d. 11h. 57m. 22s.
Io (I)	1d. 18h. 28m. 36s.
EUROPA (II)	3d. 13h. 17m. 53s.
GANYMEDE (III)	7d. 3h. 59m. 36s.
CALISTO (IV)	16d. 18h. 5m. 7s.

[For descriptive illustrated article, see "Glimpses of Jupiter," in SMITH'S PLANETARY ALMANAC for 1889; price 12 cents, post-paid.]

SATURN'S (♄) SATELLITES, 1896.

A complete re-determination of the size of Saturn and its ring system has just been finished by Prof. Barnard at the Lick Observatory. The measures correspond to the following in English miles :—

	Miles.
Outer diameter of ring	172,739.
Width of Casini's division	2,395.
Inner diameter of outer ring	149,620.
Outer diameter of inner ring	144,830.
Inner diameter of inner ring	109,530.
Inner diameter of crape ring	90,260.
Equatorial diameter of ball	76,150.
Polar diameter of ball	69,980.
Diameter of Titan (VI)	2,523.

The Satellites will be in position for observation from January 1st to about August 15th.

Sattellite.	Time of Revolution.
MIMAS (I)	0d. 22.6h.
ENCELADUS (II)	1d. 8.9h.
TETHYS (III)	1d. 21.3h.
DIONE (IV)	2d. 17.7h.
RHEA (V)	4d. 12.4h.
TITAN (VI)	15d. 23.3h.
HYPERION (VII)	21d. 7.8h.
JAPETUS (VIII)	79d. 22.0h.

URANUS' (♅) SATELLITES, 1896.

The Planet of Herschel is at opposition, May 12th. The Satellites may be seen in powerful telescopes during April and May. Their apparent distances from the Planet on May 14th are : Ariel, 14."9 ; Umbriel, 20."8 ; Titania, 34."1 ; and Oberon, 45."5.

Satellite.	Time of Revolution.
ARIEL (I)	2d. 12.48h.
UMBRIEL (II)	4d. 3.46h.
TITANIA (III)	8d. 16.94h.
OBERON (IV)	13d. 11.11h.

[For a description of Uranus and Satellites see SMITH'S PLANETARY ALMANAC for 1894 ; price 12 cents, post-paid.]

NEPTUNE'S (♆) SATELLITES, 1896.

The Planet of Adams and Le Verrier reaches Opposition on December 10th. Its Satellite has a period of 5d. 21.04h. The Satellites apparent distance from the Planet, on December 12th, 1896, is 16."9.

NO BIRTHDAY FOR SEVEN YEARS.

Persons who happened to be born on the 29th of February this year (1896) will not have another birthday until February 29th, 1904, a period of seven years.

How is this ? Let me explain. The Year 1800 was not a "leap year." The year 1900 will not be a "leap year." While February, 1892, had 29 days, and February, 1896, has 29 days, February 1900 will only have 28 days. Consequently it will be February, 1904, before another 29th of February occurs.

The year is *nearly* 365¼ days in length. I speak of days 24 hours long. It is that ¼ day over (or 6 hours) at the end of each year that gives us our "leap year" with an extra day in February every fourth year. It is because the year is *nearly* 365¼ days, and not quite, that certain days have to be omitted occasionally in order that we may not get beyond the earth's actual motion around the sun in our time-keeping. Consequently 1800 and 1900 are not "leap years." The Century years have been grouped into fours, only one in every four is "leap year." The year 2000 will be the next Century "leap year."

To still better understand the case it may be explained that the actual time taken by the Earth to complete one revolution about the Sun (year) is 365 days, 5 hours, 48 minutes, 46 seconds. When we add an extra day every four years for that 5 hours, 48 minutes, 46 seconds, we make each year 365 days and 6 hours in length. But this is 11 minutes and 14 seconds too much. In order to correct this slight error, three twenty-ninths of February are omitted in four centuries. That brings us very close to the exact measure.

Still, this reduction by the four hundredth part of three days (10 minutes 46 seconds) leaves the year too long by 26 seconds. How do the astronomers manage with this slight surplus? They do no let it pile up and ultimately confuse everything and everybody. They have a place for it. Having found that it amounts to nearly 86,400 (24 hours) in the course of 3,323 years, they have arranged for the present "style" to continue in vogue for thirty centuries when an extra day will be dropped and there will have to be a year only 364 days in length. -

THE PSYCHOLOGY OF THE WEATHER.

A new and what must prove to be an interesting field for investigation has just been suggested, namely, that of the psychology of the weather. Experimenters and others engaged in mental tasks of an exacting description have found faulty deductions and misconceptions to be the result of their work in damp, foggy weather, or on days in which the air was charged with electricity and thunderstorms were impending. Indeed, deductions which seemed clear at these times appeared later to be filled with error. An actuary in a large insurance company is obliged to stop work at such times, because he finds that he makes so many mistakes. A further confirmatory fact is that in large factories from 10 to 20 percent less work is accomplished on damp days and days of threatening storm than when the weather is fine. And this is further very clear, that a minister often finds his congregation greatly affected by the condition of the atmosphere. It affords a curious example of the effect of the physical in the region of the intellectual and of the spiritual as well.—*Selected.*

GENERAL FORECAST, 1896.

The weather is .by no means a subject which should be regarded merely as a matter of conversation for the multitudes of people who find it difficult to talk about anything else. The subject is, in reality, one of great and paramount importance ;· of far more importance than many others which occupy the time and the thoughts of the public ; and it is only neglected on account of the obscurity behind which the causes of weather changes have been hitherto concealed, and of the consequent apparent futility of discussing them. If any scientific investigation could bring the subject of weather changes within the region of positive knowledge, so that unalterable forecasts might be made concerning them, it would at once become manifest that scarcely any other subject could vie with them in universality of interest. The power of foreseeing the weather of the next few days would do much, the power of foreseeing the weather of the next season would do almost everything, to take away from agriculture the uncertainty which is now its greatest hindrance ; and a bad harvest season would then no longer, as at present, entail upon the world a loss which must be estimated by millions.

But it takes all kinds of people to make a world, and if the scoffers and "I told you so" class will sneer at an error, the many kind words of encouragement which I have received is not forgotten ; and with this expression of thanks, I submit the general probabilities for 1896.

JANUARY.

A stormy month. Some wild, stormy days, and severe, cold "dips," with a mild, rainy, sleety period. Opening with fair weather, there will be a stormy spell in each week of the month, moderating to clear, cold, bracing weather. The feature of this month will be its blustery, unsettled state, with mean temperature above the average, the closing days stormy and cold.

FEBRUARY.

A cold, stormy month, with considerable precipitation of snow and rain. Entering blustery and disagreeable, the second week will give a severe and protracted dip of extreme weather; the following week heavy gales on the Atlantic seaboard and Lakes, with much snow and rains, and the closing week stormy and cold, with a mild spell at middle and end.

MARCH.

An old-fashioned "lion-like" month up to about 10th inst., with severe storms, snow blockades, generally cold zero weather in all sections, and disastrous gales on Atlantic coast; after which a general break-up is probable, and mild weather set in, the remaining days giving promise of being "lamb-like" in the extreme, the month closing cloudy, with snow.

APRIL.

A fickle, wayward month, with alternate gleams of sunshine and cloudy weather, the latter predominating. The first and second weeks will likely prove very rainy, but fairly warm; the third cool to cold, with high winds; the fourth threatening and dark, with abundance of rain and hail, the month closing with rapid changes, and foggy, misty, squally weather.

MAY.

A cold, backward month as a whole, with abnormal ranges of temperature from frost-line to summer heat, very heavy rains, cool to cold weather, high winds and sharp frosts.

JUNE.

Enters windy, but fair, warm, pleasant summer weather, the second week promising to be warm to cool, with high winds, some heavy rains and slight frosts; the third with showers and high winds, changing to hot and sultry; and the fourth rainy and unsettled, month closing fine and favorable.

JULY.

A showery month, with some damaging thunderstorms in he early and latter part. Entering warm and hot, the second week promises a sultry term, tempered at close with cool showers; a cool spell about 18th, followed by a dull cloudy week, hot at close, month ending very warm and sultry, with severe thunderstorm.

AUGUST.

A glance at the weekly probabilities for this month will give an idea of its mixed features, and will show more than the usual August rain. The week ending the 22nd inst. will be far and away the pleasantest period of the month, though the succeeding days will have more than a fair share of fine weather, with showers; and a cool term.

SEPTEMBER.

A mild, pleasant, dry month, with high winds; frosts probable about the close of second week; rains in first and second weeks, but balance of month fine; very favourable for exhibitions and out door work generally.

OCTOBER.

A cold, bleak month, with blustery high winds and considerable precipitation of snow, sleet, and rain; rough weather on Lakes and Atlantic coast about middle of month, and a marked mild "Indian summer" spell in closing week.

NOVEMBER.

A month of stormy, boisterous weather. Every week of this month will have its particular storm, except the first, which gives promise of being fairly warm, as does also the last three or four days of the month.

DECEMBER.

Opens with high winds, rain or snow; a stormy downfall of rain or sleet in second week, but clear and mild at close. From 13th to 26th gives promise of mild, soft, pleasant weather, with a cold snap about 23rd; month ending colder, with high winds.

JAMES H. OXLEY.

MONTREAL, *August 1st*, 1895.

1st Month, 1896. 31 Days.	JANUARY.	☉ enters ♒ 20d. 7h. mo

Moon's Phases	Day.	BOSTON.	MONTREAL.	WASHINGTON	CHICAGO.	WINNIPEG.
☾ L.Q.	7	10.44 mo.	10.30 mo.	10.17 mo.	9.35 mo.	8.57 mo.
● N.M.	14	5.38 ev.	5.24 ev.	5.11 ev.	4.29 ev.	3.51 ev.
☽ F.Q.	22	10.01 ev.	9.47 ev.	9.34 ev.	8.52 ev.	8.14 ev.
☺ F.M.	30	4.14 mo.	4.00 mo.	3.47 mo.	3.05 mo.	2.27 mo.

DAYS.		WEATHER FORECAST.	MONTREAL.					
			THE SUN				THE MOON	
M.	W.		Slow.	Rises.	Sets.		Zod.	Souths.
			M.	H. M.	H. M.			H. M.
1	We.	**NEW YEARS DAY.**	3	7 42	4 27		♋	Morn
2	Th.	Fair, changing to snow in Northern and	4	7 41	4 28		♌	1 26
3	Fr.		4	7 41	4 29		♌	2 23
4	Sat.	Eastern sections, rain and sleet South	5	7 41	4 30		♍	3 15

(1) **2nd Sunday after Christmas.** (Day's length, 8h. 51m.) ☿ in ♐								
5	Su.		5	7 40	4 31		♍	4 04
6	Mo.	**EPIPHANY.**	6	7 40	4 32		♎	4 53
7	Tu.		6	7 39	4 33		♎	5 41
8	We.	Stormy and blustery from 5th to 9th—	7	7 39	4 34		♎	6 30
9	Th.	Drifts in North-West—Moderating to fine,	7	7 39	4 35		♏	7 21
10	Fr.	with wind and snow—Changeable	8	7 38	4 36		♏	8 15
11	Sat.		8	7 38	4 37		♐	9 12

(2) **1st Sunday after Epiphany.** (Day's length, 9h. 01m.) ♀ in ♍								
12	Su.		9	7 37	4 38		♐	10 10
13	Mo.		9	7 37	4 40		♑	11 06
14	Tu.	Windy—Cold and very unsettled period	9	7 36	4 41		♑	Eve.
15	We.		10	7 36	4 42		♒	0 51
16	Th.	—Some very low temperatures recorded.	10	7 35	4 43		♒	1 37
17	Fr.		10	7 35	4 44		♓	2 20
18	Sat.		11	7 34	4 46		♓	3 01

(3) **2nd Sunday after Epiphany.** (Day's length, 9h. 14m.) ♂ in ♐								
19	Su.		11	7 34	4 48		♓	3 40
20	Mo.		11	7 33	4 49		♈	4 19
21	Tu.	Gusty and cold—Stormy—Cold—Unset-	12	7 32	4 51		♈	4 59
22	We.		12	7 31	4 52		♈	5 40
23	Th.	tled and blustery.	12	7 30	4 54		♉	6 25
24	Fr.		12	7 29	4 55		♉	7 14
25	Sat.	**Conversion of St. Paul.**	13	7 28	4 56		♊	8 08

(4) **3rd Sunday after Epiphany.** (Day's length, 9h. 30m.) ♃ in ♋								
26	Su.		13	7 27	4 57		♊	9 06
27	Mo.	Stormy, with rapid changes and flurries	13	7 26	4 58		♋	10 07
28	Tu.		13	7 25	4 59		♋	11 08
29	We.	of snow and sleet—Cloudy and boisterous	13	7 24	5 01		♌	Morn
30	Th.	East, cold weather West.	14	7 23	5 03		♌	0 07
31	Fr.		14	7 22	5 04		♍	1 03

☾ In this month the Mornings increase 20 min and the Afternoons 37 min.

PLANETS IN JANUARY, 1896.

MONTREAL MEAN TIME.

*ON MERIDIAN (SOUTH).	Jan. 1st.	Jan. 8th.	Jan. 16th.	Jan. 24th.
Mercury .... ☿	0 35 ev.	0 57 ev.	1 18 ev.	1 26 ev.
Venus ...... ♀	8 56 mo.	9 02 mo.	9 10 mo.	9 19 mo.
Mars .... ♂	10 09 mo.	10 04 mo.	9 58 mo.	9 51 mo.
Jupiter .... ♃	1 56 mo.	1 26 mo.	0 50 mo.	0 14 mo.
Saturn ..... ♄	8 17 mo.	7 51 mo.	7 22 mo.	6 53 mo.
Uranus .... ♅	8 41 mo.	8 14 mo.	7 44 mo.	7 14 mo.
Neptune ... ♆	10 15 ev.	9 46 ev.	9 14 ev.	8 42 ev.

[* Planets "Southing" between noon and midnight are "Evening stars"; planets "Southing" between midnight and noon are "Morning stars." The time of "Southing" is the time at which a heavenly body passes the meridian, and is so called because it is then due South. It is then also at its greatest altitude above the horizon.]

THE PLANETS.—MERCURY is at Greatest Elongation East of the Sun on the 24th at 0h. 13m. mo., when he is visible after sunset in the evening sky; in Perihelion (nearest point of his orbit to the Sun) on the 28th at 7h. ev., and Stationary amongst the Stars on the 30th at 2h. mo. JUPITER is at greatest brilliancy on the 24th at 8h. mo.

THE MOON.—Is near Jupiter on the 2nd at 0h. 09m. ev.; passes Saturn on the 9th at 6h. 44m. ev. ; is close to Uranus on the 10th at 4h. 31m. mo. ; leaves Venus behind on the celestial course at 6h. 19m. mo. on the 11th. ; is 4° 35' S. of Mars on the 12th at 6h. 18m. mo., and only 32' S. of Mercury on the 16th at 2h. 41m. mo. She is 6° 36' N. of Neptune on the 26th at 8h. 21m. mo., and passes close to Jupiter on the 29th at 4h. 24m. ev.

PERIGEE: 3rd, 11h. 13m. ev.; APOGEE: 19th, 11h. 20m. ev.; PERIGEE: 31st, 9h. ev.

THE STARS.—[Commenced in 1891 issue. Under this head, it is my intention to continue each year, until the whole visible star sphere has been briefly described. In no case will a Constellation, Group, Cluster, or Star be twice dealt with. Students should, therefore, preserve back numbers.]

Eridanus, "the River Po," occupies a large and very irregular space. It is not easy to trace all its supposed windings. It has an entire length of about 130°. It is divided into two sections, the North and the South. That portion lying between *Orion* and *Cetus* is called the "Northern Stream," the rest is termed the "Southern Stream." The "Northern Stream" commences near *Rigel* in *Orion*.

2nd Month, 1896.
29 Days.

FEBRUARY.

☉ enters ♓
18d. 8h. ev.

Moon's Phases	Day.	BOSTON.	MONTREAL.	WASHINGTON	CHICAGO.	WINNIPEG.
☾ L.Q.	5	7.57 ev.	7.43 ev.	7.30 ev.	6.48 ev.	6.10 ev.
● N.M.	13	11.31 mo.	11.17 mo.	11.04 mo.	10.22 mo.	9.44 mo.
☽ F.Q.	21	4.33 ev.	4.19 ev.	4.06 ev.	3.24 ev.	2.46 ev.
☺ F.M.	28	3.10 ev.	2.56 ev.	2.43 ev.	2.01 ev.	1.23 ev.

DAYS. M.	W.	WEATHER FORECAST.	MONTREAL. —THE SUN— Slow. M.	Rises. H. M.	Sets. H. M.	THE MOON Zod.	Souths. H. M.
1	Sat.	Variable, unpleasant.	14	7 21	5 06	♍	Morn
(5) Septuagesima Sunday.		(Day's length, 9h. 48m.) ♄ in ♎					
2	Su.	**CANDLEMAS.**	14	7 20	5 08	♍	2 46
3	Mo.		14	7 19	5 09	♎	3 36
4	Tu.	Blustery, disagreeable weather—Moderat-	14	7 18	5 11	♎	4 26
5	We.		14	7 17	5 12	♏	5 17
6	Th.	ing to fine and cloudy—Week closes cold.	14	7 16	5 14	♏	6 11
7	Fr.		14	7 14	5 15	♐	7 07
8	Sat.		14	7 13	5 17	♐	8 04
(6) Sexagesima Sunday.		(Day's length, 10h. 06m.) ♅ in ♎					
9	Su.		14	7 12	5 18	♑	9 01
10	Mo.	A severe and protracted "dip" of ex-	14	7 10	5 19	♑	9 55
11	Tu.	treme weather—Very low temperatures—	14	7 09	5 21	♒	10 46
12	We.	Stormy—Very cold.	14	7 07	5 22	♒	11 33
13	Th.		14	7 06	5 24	♒	Eve.
14	Fr.	**ST. VALENTINE.**	14	7 04	5 25	♓	0 58
15	Sat.		14	7 02	5 27	♓	1 38
(7) Quinquagesima Sunday.		(Day's length, 10h. 27m.) ♆ in ♉					
16	Su.	Heavy gales on Atlantic seaboard—	14	7 01	5 28	♓	2 17
17	Mo.		14	6 59	5 30	♈	2 56
18	Tu.	**SHROVE TUESDAY.**	14	6 58	5 31	♈	3 36
19	We.	**ASH WEDNESDAY.**	14	6 56	5 33	♉	4 20
20	Th.	Abundant snow and rain (floods probable)	14	6 54	5 34	♉	5 04
21	Fr.	—Stormy.	14	6 53	5 36	♉	5 57
22	Sat.	**Washington born, 1732.**	14	6 51	5 37	♊	6 51
(8) Quadragesima Sunday.		(Day's length, 10h. 49m.) ☿ in ♑					
23	Su.		14	6 50	5 39	♊	7 49
24	Mo.	Stormy, cold and blustery, with snow—	13	6 48	5 40	♋	8 49
25	Tu.		13	6 47	5 41	♋	9 48
26	We.	Moderating to fine—Month closes with	13	6 45	5 43	♌	10 45
27	Th.		13	6 44	5 45	♌	11 39
28	Fr.	snow or rain—Milder.	13	6 43	5 46	♍	Morn
29	Sat.		13	6 42	5 47	♍	0 32

☾ In this month the Mornings increase 39 min. and the Afternoons 41 min.
The Moon's place is given in the Zodiac "Sign" for the convenience of farmers and gardeners. The places of the planets refer to the Zodiacal "Constellations."

PLANETS IN FEBRUARY, 1896.

MONTREAL MEAN TIME.

ON MERIDIAN (SOUTH).	Feb. 1st.	Feb. 8th.	Feb. 16th.	Feb. 24th.
Mercury ...... ☿	1 02 ev.	0 10 ev.	11 09 mo.	10 37 mo.
Venus .... ♀	9 29 mo.	9 38 mo.	9 48 mo.	9 58 mo.
Mars .... ♂	9 46 mo.	9 41 mo.	9 35 mo.	9 29 mo.
Jupiter .... ♃	11 34 ev.	11 03 ev.	10 28 ev.	9 53 ev.
Saturn .... ♄	6 21 mo.	5 56 mo.	5 25 mo.	4 54 mo.
Uranus .... ♅	6 43 mo.	6 15 mo.	5 44 mo.	5 13 mo.
Neptune ...... ♆	8 10 ev.	7 42 ev.	7 10 ev.	6 39 ev.

THE PLANETS.—MERCURY reaches Inferior Conjunction with the Sun on the 8th at 1h. ev., when he passes between that luminary and the Earth; he is Stationary among the Stars on the 20th at 1h. ev. VENUS and Mars are in Conjunction (Venus 1° 38′ N.) on the 9th at 3h. ev. SATURN is 90° from the Sun (Quadrature) on the 7th at 7h. ev.; when he is overhead at 6h. mo.; he is Stationary on the 27th at 7h. mo. URANUS is 90° from the Sun (and overhead at 6h. mo.) on the 13th at 9h. mo. He is Stationary on the 27th at 4h. ev. NEPTUNE is Stationary on the 24th at 4h. ev.

THE MOON.—Passes 7° 46′ S. of Saturn on the 6th at 3h. 52m. mo.; is near Uranus the same da y(5° 40′ S.) at 11h. 23m. mo.; is in Conjunction with Mars (3° 27′ S.) on the 10th at 2h. 29m. mo.; passes 5° 3′ S. of Venus the same day at 2h. 57m. mo.; leaves Mercury behind on the 12th at 1h. 10m. ev.; is 6° 39′ N. of Neptune on the 22nd at 5h. 08m. ev., and is 2° 18′ N. of Jupiter on the 25th at 10h. 16m. ev.

APOGEE: 16th, 3h. ev.; PERIGEE- 29th, 6h. 30m. mo.; ECLIPSED: 28th, (see page 17).

THE STARS.—In *Canis Major*, about 4° below *Sirius*. In R.A. 6h. 42m., Decl. 20° 37′ S. will be found a superb cluster of stars, visible to the unaided eye. Its larger Stars are arranged in curves, and there is a ruddy Star near the centre. Another beautiful cluster will be found in R.A. 7h. 12m., Decl. 15° 25′ S.; melting away into a very rich neighborhood, as if the Galaxy were approaching the observer. The Stars in this cluster are nearly all of the tenth magnitude.

3rd Month, 1896. 31 Days.	MARCH.	☉ enters ♈ 19d. 9h. ev

Moon's Phase:	Day.	BOSTON.	MONTREAL.	WASHINGTON	CHICAGO.	WINNIPEG.
☾ L.Q.	6	6.48 mo.	6.34 mo.	6.21 mo.	5.39 mo.	5.01 mo.
● N.M.	14	6.07 mo.	5.53 mo.	5.40 mo.	4.58 mo.	4.20 mo.
☽ F.Q.	22	7.15 mo.	7.01 mo.	6.48 mo.	6.06 mo.	5.28 mo.
☺ F.M.	27-28	0.40 mo.	0.26 mo.	0.13 mo.	11.31 ev.	10.53 ev.

DAYS.	WEATHER FORECAST.	MONTREAL.			
		THE SUN			THE MOON
M. | W.		Slow	Rises.	Sets.	Zod. Souths.

(9) 2nd Sunday in Lent. (Day's length, 11h. 08m.) ♀ in ♑

		M.	H. M.	H. M.		H. M.
1 Su.	ST. DAVID.	12	6 40	5 48	♎	Morn
2 Mo.		12	6 39	5 49	♎	2 15
3 Tu.	Comes in cold, stormy and "lion like"	12	6 37	5 50	♏	3 08
4 We.	—Snow blockades N. and N.W.—Sleet	12	6 35	5 51	♏	4 03
5 Th.	and snow W.—Generally cold weather in	11	6 33	5 53	♐	5 00
6 Fr.	all sections—Storms on Atlantic Coast.	11	6 31	5 54	♐	5 59
7 Sat.		11	6 29	5 55	♑	6 56

(10) 3rd Sunday in Lent. (Day's length, 11h. 30m.) ♂ in ♑

8 Su.		11	6 27	5 57	♑	7 51
9 Mo.	Stormy period, probably lasting up to	10	6 25	5 58	♒	8 43
10 Tu.		10	6 23	6 00	♒	9 31
11 We.	10th inst.—Indications of windy, but fine	10	6 21	6 01	♒	10 16
12 Th.		10	6 19	6 02	♓	10 57
13 Fr.	and pleasant term.	9	6 17	6 03	♓	11 37
14 Sat.		9	6 15	6 04	♓	Eve.

(11) 4th Sunday in Lent. (Day's length, 11h. 54m.) ♃ in ♋

15 Su.	Mild spell of clear, spring-like weather	9	6 13	6 06	♈	0 55
16 Mo.		9	6 11	6 07	♈	1 35
17 Tu.	ST. PATRICK.	8	6 09	6 08	♈	2 17
18 We.		8	6 07	6 10	♉	3 02
19 Th.	—Warm for season—Brief stormy period	8	6 06	6 11	♉	3 51
20 Fr.	—Mild and fine.	7	6 04	6 13	♊	4 43
21 Sat.		7	6 02	6 14	♊	5 38

(12) 5th Sunday in Lent. (Day's length, 12h. 15m.) ♄ in ♎

22 Su.		7	6 00	6 15	♋	6 35
23 Mo.	Clear—Milder—Finer weather—Threat-	6	5 58	6 16	♋	7 33
24 Tu.		6	5 56	6 18	♌	8 29
25 We.	ANNUNCIATION.	6	5 54	6 19	♌	9 23
26 Th.		5	5 52	6 20	♍	10 15
27 Fr.	ening—Stormy, but mild.	5	5 50	6 21	♍	11 07
28 Sat.		5	5 48	6 23	♎	11 59

(13) Palm Sunday. (Day's length, 12h. 37m.) ♅ in ♎

29 Su.		5	5 47	6 24	♎	Morn
30 Mo.	Month closes cloudy with snows.	4	5 45	6 26	♏	0 52
31 Tu.		4	5 43	6 27	♏	1 48

In this month the Mornings increase 57 min. and the Afternoons 39 min.

PLANETS IN MARCH, 1896.

MONTREAL MEAN TIME.

ON MERIDIAN (SOUTH).	Mar. 1st.	Mar. 8th.	Mar. 16th.	Mar. 24th.
Mercury ...... ☿	10 28 mo.	10 29 mo.	10 38 mo.	10 51 mo.
Venus .... ♀	10 04 mo.	10 11 mo.	10 19 mo.	10 25 mo.
Mars .... ♂	9 24 mo.	9 19 mo.	9 12 mo.	9 05 mo.
Jupiter .... ♃	9 27 ev.	8 58 ev.	8 25 ev.	7 53 ev.
Saturn .... ♄	4 30 mo.	4 02 mo.	3 30 mo.	2 57 mo.
Uranus .... ♅	4 50 mo.	4 22 mo.	3 50 mo.	3 18 mo.
Neptune ..... ♆	6 14 ev.	5 49 ev.	5 17 ev.	4 47 ev.

THE PLANETS.—MERCURY reaches Gre t Elongation West on the 5th at 3h. ev., when he is 27° 20' from the Sun and easily seen in the morning sky before sunrise ; he passes Aphelion (farthest from the Sun) on the 12th at 6h. ev. VENUS is in very close Conjunction (6' S.) of the Star *Mu Capricorni* on the 14th at 8h. mo. (best seen prior to sunrise). JUPITER is Stationary at 7h. ev. on the 24th. NEPTUNE reaches Quadrature (90° from the Sun) at 3h. mo. on the 5th, and is overhead at 6h. ev.

THE MOON.—Is 7° 54' S. of Saturn on the 4th at 10h. 23m. mo. ; is 5° 42' S. of Uranus the same day at 6h. 24m. ev. ; passes 1° 37' S. of Mars on the 10th at 2h. 01m.. ; is very close to Venus (35' S.) on the 11th at 9h. 24m. mo. ; in Conjunction with Mercury (42' N.) the same evening at 7h. 40m. ; passes 6° 33' N. of Neptune on the 21st at 0h. 41m. mo. ; passes Jupiter (2° 19' N.) on the 24th at 5h. 50m., and reaches Conjunction with Saturn for the second time this month on the 31st at 6h. 19m. ev.

APOGEE : 14th, 8h. 20m. ev. ; PERIGEE : 28th, 6h. 20m.

THE STARS.—The clusters and nebulæ in *Argo Navis* well repay careful examination. A couple of these were described in last issue. Other interesting objects will be found, as follows : In R.A. 7h. 37m., Decl. 17° 55' S., is a Planetary Nebula, quite bright, of a pale bluish white. In low powers it appears like a dull eighth magnitude Star, with high powers it becomes smaller, but brilliant, yet undefined, surrounded with a very faint haze. It is in a very rich neighborhood. The Earl of Rosse notes a red star of about the ninth magnitude "following" it.

4th Month, 1896.
30 Days.

APRIL.

☉ enters ♉
19d 10h. mo.

Moon's Phases	Day.	BOSTON.	MONTREAL.	WASHINGTON	CHICAGO.	WINNIPEG.
☾ L.Q.	4	7.43 ev.	7.29 ev.	7.16 ev.	6.34 ev.	5.56 ev.
● N.M.	12	11.42 ev.	11.28 ev.	11.15 ev.	10.33 ev.	9.55 ev.
☽ F.Q.	20	6.06 ev.	5.52 ev.	5.39 ev.	4.57 ev.	4.19 ev.
○ F.M.	27	9.06 mo.	8.52 mo.	8.39 mo.	7.57 mo.	7.19 mo

DAYS.		WEATHER FORECAST.	MONTREAL.							
			—THE SUN—					THE MOON		
M.	W.		Slow	Rises.		Sets.		Zod.	Souths	
			M.	H.	M.	H.	M.		H.	M.
1	We.	Fair, with high winds—Rain—Unsettled.	4	5	41	6	28	♏	Morn	
2	Th.		3	5	40	6	29	♐	3	47
3	Fr.	**GOOD FRIDAY.**	3	5	38	6	31	♐	4	47
4	Sat.		3	5	36	6	32	♑	5	45
(14) **Easter Sunday.**		(Day's length, 12h 59m.) ☿ in ♓								
5	Su.		2	5	34	6	33	♑	6	39
6	Mo.		2	5	32	6	34	♒	7	29
7	Tu.	Gusty, unsettled and rainy—Warm show-	2	5	30	6	35	♒	8	14
8	We.		2	5	28	6	37	♓	8	57
9	Th.	ers—Continued rains.	1	5	26	6	38	♓	9	37
10	Fr.		1	5	24	6	39	♓	10	16
11	Sat.		1	5	22	6	40	♈	10	55
(15) **Low Sunday.**		(Day's length, 13h. 22m.) ♀ in ♓								
12	Su.		1	5	20	6	42	♈	11	35
13	Mo.	Rainy—Cool to cold—Gusty, variable	0	5	19	6	43	♈	Eve.	
14	Tu.		0	5	17	6	45	♉	1	01
15	We.	weather, with scattered showers—Windy,	fast	5	15	6	46	♉	1	48
16	Th.		0	5	13	6	47	♊	2	39
17	Fr.	unsettled.	1	5	11	6	48	♊	3	33
18	Sat.		1	5	10	6	50	♋	4	29
(16) **2nd Sunday after Easter.**		(Day's length, 13h. 43m.) ♂ in ♒								
19	Su.		1	5	08	6	51	♋	5	25
20	Mo.	Rain or hail—Dark, cloudy, unsettled—	1	5	07	6	52	♌	6	20
21	Tu.	Variable and gusty—Heavy rains.	2	5	05	6	53	♌	7	13
22	We.		2	5	03	6	54	♌	8	04
23	Th.	**ST. GEORGE.**	2	5	02	6	56	♍	8	54
24	Fr.		2	5	00	6	57	♍	9	44
25	Sat.	**ST. MARK.**	2	4	59	6	58	♎	10	36
(17) **3rd Sunday after Easter.**		(Day's length, 14h. 02m.) ♃ in ♋								
26	Su.	Extreme temperatures—Rapid changes	2	4	57	6	59	♎	11	30
27	Mo.	from heat to cold and vice-versâ—Foggy	3	4	56	7	01	♏	Morn	
28	Tu.	and misty on Atlantic seaboard—Some	3	4	54	7	02	♏	0	27
29	We.	sudden squalls.	3	4	52	7	04	♐	1	28
30	Th.		3	4	50	7	05	♐	2	30

In this month the Mornings increase 51 min. and the Afternoons 37 min.

PLANETS IN APRIL, 1896.

MONTREAL MEAN TIME.

ON MERIDIAN (SOUTH).	April 1st.	April 8th.	April 16th.	April 24th.
Mercury ...... ☿	11 09 mo.	11 27 mo.	11 54 mo.	0 26 ev.
Venus .... ♀	10 30 mo.	10 34 mo.	10 39 mo.	10 44 mo.
Mars .... ♂	8 59 mo.	8 51 mo.	8 43 mo.	8 34 mo.
Jupiter .... ♃	7 22 ev.	6 56 ev.	6 26 ev.	5 58 ev.
Saturn .... ♄	2 25 mo.	1 56 mo.	1 22 mo.	0 48 mo.
Uranus .... ♅	2 46 mo.	2 17 mo.	1 45 mo.	1 12 mo.
Neptune ...... ♆	4 16 ev.	3 49 ev.	3 18 ev.	2 48 ev.

THE PLANETS.—MERCURY is in Superior Conjunction with the Sun on the 18th at 0h. mo., and in Perihelion on the 25th at 6h. ev. VENUS makes her Aphelion passage on the 1st at 8h. ev. JUPITER is 90° from the Sun at noon on the 19th, when he is overhead at 6h. ev.

THE MOON.—Will be 5° 36' S. of Uranus on the 1st at 2h. 42m. mo.; less than 1° N. of Mars on the 8th at 5h. 24m. mo.; near Venus on the 10th at 11h. 02m. ev.; 5° 30' N. of Mercury on the 12th at 3h. 08m. mo.; near Neptune on the 17th at 7h. 27m. mo.; passes 2° 2' N. of Jupiter on the 20th at 3h. 05m.; is 7° 48' S. of Saturn on the 28th at 2h. 13m. mo., and 5° 29' S. of Uranus the same day at 11h. 43m. mo.

APOGEE: 10th, 10h. 35m. ev.; PERIGEE: 26th, 4h. 19m. mo.

THE STARS.—A very fine Planetary Nebula will be found in the Constellation *Hydra*. Its R.A. is 10h. 19m., Decl. 18° 2' S. (about 2° South of *Mu Hydræ*). This object somewhat resembles the Planet Jupiter in size, equability of light and color. It is a little elliptical in shape and bears high powers. Herschel failed to resolve it into Stars. Secchi, in the clear sky of Italy, with a beautiful glass and a power of 1,000, reported it "an unique object," describing it as having within a circular nebulosity two clusters connected by two semi-circular arches of Stars, forming a sparkling ring, with one Star on the hazy groundwork forming the centre. D'Arrest made out two nuclei near the limit. Huggins saw an oval ring surrounded by a broad faint nebulosity, but having a gaseous spectrum. The Star points cannot in consequence be solid matter.

5th Month, 1896. 31 Days.	MAY.	☉ enters ♊ 20d. 10h. mo.

Moon's Phases	Day.	BOSTON.	MONTREAL.	WASHINGTON	CHICAGO.	WINNIPEG.
☾ L.Q.	4	10.44 mo.	10.30 mo.	10.17 mo.	9.35 mo.	8.57 mo.
● N.M.	12	3.05 ev.	2.51 ev.	2.38 ev.	1.56 ev.	1.18 ev.
☽ F.Q.	18-19	1.40 mo.	1.26 mo.	1.13 mo.	0.31 mo.	11.53 ev.
☺ F.M.	26	5.15 ev.	5.01 ev.	4.48 ev.	4.06 ev.	3.28 ev.

DAYS. M. W.	WEATHER FORECAST.	MONTREAL. THE SUN Fast. Rises. Sets.	THE MOON Zod. Souths.
1 Fr.	**MAY DAY.**	3 4 49 7 06	♑ Morn
2 Sat.	Enters cold and moist.	3 4 47 7 07	♑ 4 29

(18) 4th Sunday after Easter. (Day's length, 14h. 23m.) ♄ in ♎

3 Su.		3 4 46 7 09	♒ 5 22
4 Mo.		3 4 44 7 10	♒ 6 10
5 Tu.	Windy and unsettled—Rainy and misty,	4 4 43 7 11	♓ 6 54
6 We.		4 4 42 7 12	♓ 7 35
7 Th.	with showers—Finer.	4 4 40 7 13	♓ 8 15
8 Fr.		4 4 39 7 14	♈ 8 54
9 Sat.		4 4 37 7 16	♈ 9 33

(19) Rogation Sunday. (Day's length, 14h. 41m.) ♅ in ♎

10 Su.		4 4 36 7 17	♈ 10 14
11 Mo.	Dark, cold and showery — Stormy —	4 4 35 7 18	♉ 10 58
12 Tu.	Heavy rains and sleet—Milder—Showers	4 4 34 7 19	♉ 11 44
13 We.		4 4 33 7 21	♊ Eve.
14 Th.	**ASCENSION DAY.**	4 4 31 7 22	♊ 1 29
15 Fr.	—Gusty winds.	4 4 30 7 23	♊ 2 25
16 Sat.		4 4 29 7 24	♋ 3 21

(20) Sunday after Ascension. (Day's length, 14h. 57m.) ☿ in ♉

17 Su.	**Montreal founded, 1642.**	4 4 28 7 25	♋ 4 16
18 Mo.		4 4 27 7 26	♌ 5 08
19 Tu.	Cool to cold—Rainy, disagreeable—	4 4 26 7 27	♌ 5 59
20 We.		4 4 25 7 28	♍ 6 47
21 Th.	Gusty, variable and unsettled period.	4 4 24 7 29	♍ 7 36
22 Fr.		3 4 23 7 30	♎ 8 25
23 Sat.		3 4 22 7 31	♎ 9 16

(21) Whit Sunday (Pentecost). (Day's length, 15h. 11m.) ♀ in ♉

24 Su.	**Queen Victoria born, 1819.**	3 4 21 7 32	♏ 10 11
25 Mo.		3 4 20 7 33	♏ 11 09
26 Tu.	Cold and rainy—Sharp frosts—Variable,	3 4 19 7 34	♐ Morn
27 We.		3 4 19 7 35	♐ 0 11
28 Th.	strong winds.	3 4 18 7 36	♑ 1 13
29 Fr.		3 4 18 7 37	♑ 2 14
30 Sat.	**DECORATION DAY.**	3 4 17 7 38	♒ 3 10

(22) Trinity Sunday. (Day's length, 15h. 23m.) ♂ in ♓

31 Su.	Clear—Cool winds.	2 4 16 7 39	♒ 4 01

In this month the Mornings increase 33 min. and the Afternoons 33 min.

PLANETS IN MAY, 1896.

MONTREAL MEAN TIME.

ON MERIDIAN (SOUTH).	May 1st.	May 8th.	May 16th.	May 24th.
Mercury .... ☿	0 55 ev.	1 17 ev.	1 29 ev.	1 21 ev.
Venus ...... ♀	10 48 mo.	10 53 mo.	10 59 mo.	11 06 mo.
Mars .... ♂	8 27 mo.	8 19 mo.	8 09 mo.	8 00 mo.
Jupiter ..... ♃	5 34 ev.	5 09 ev.	4 42 ev.	4 16 ev.
Saturn ...... ♄	0 19 mo.	11 45 ev.	11 11 ev.	10 38 ev.
Uranus ..... ♅	0 44 mo.	0 15 mo.	11 38 ev.*	11 05 ev.
Neptune .... ♆	2 21 ev.	1 55 ev.	1 25 ev.	0 55 ev.

THE PLANETS.—MERCURY and Neptune are in Conjunction on the 15th at 11h. mo., when Mercury is 3° 45' N. of his far away brother; the pair should be seen in a glass in the evening sky, Mercury on the following day reaching "Greatest Elongation East" of the Sun, when he is 22° 9' from that luminary. The little Planet is Stationary on the 29th at 8h. mo. VENUS, still prominent in the morning sky, is in very close Conjunction with the Star *Omicron Piscium* (10' N.) on the 3rd at 11h. ev.(best seen on the mornings of the 3rd and 4th before sunrise). SATURN is at his brightest on the 5th, when he is overhead at midnight, having passed Opposition at 4h. ev. URANUS reaches Opposition on the 12th at 1h. ev., when he should be seen with the unaided eye on the meridian at midnight as a Star of the fifth magnitude. NEPTUNE is 3° 45' S. of Mercury on the 15th at 11h. mo.

THE MOON.—Passes 3° 37' N. of Mars on the 7th at 11h. 16m. mo.; is near Venus on the 11th at 9h. 27m. mo.; close to Mercury at 0h. 54m. ev. on the 14th; 6° 11' N. of Neptune the same day at 2h. 40m. ev.; alongside Jupiter on the 18th at 2h. 23m. mo; leaves Saturn behind on the 25th at 9h. 07m. mo., and passes Uranus the same day at 8h. 05m. ev.

APOGEE; 8th, 10h. 50m. mo.; PERIGEE: 24th, 6h. 25m. mo.

THE STARS.—In *Ursa Major* will be found a large, pale, planetary nebula; sometimes called the "Owl Nebula," a very remarkable object. R.A. 11h. 8m.; Decl. 55° 40' N. This nebula, if not farther away than the nearest fixed stars, is large enough to equal the orbit of Neptune seven times over.

6th Month, 1896.
30 Days.

JUNE.

☉ enters ♋
20d. 5h. ev.

Moon's Phases	Day.	BOSTON.	MONTREAL.	WASHINGTON	CHICAGO.	WINNIPEG.
☾ L.Q.	3	3.21 mo.	3.07 mo.	2.54 mo.	2.12 mo.	1.34 mo.
● N.M.	11	4.02 mo.	3.48 mo.	3.35 mo.	2.53 mo.	2.15 mo.
☽ F.Q.	18	6.59 mo.	6.45 mo.	6.32 mo.	5.50 mo.	5.12 mo.
☺ F.M.	25	2.14 mo.	2.00 mo.	1.47 mo.	1.05 mo.	0.27 mo.

DAYS.		WEATHER FORECAST.	MONTREAL.							
			THE SUN					THE MOON		
M.	W.		Fast.	Rises.		Sets.		Zod.	Souths.	
			M.	H.	M.	H.	M.		H.	M.
1	Mo.		2	4	16	7	40	♒	Morn	
2	Tu.	Opens windy, but fair and warm—Fine	2	4	15	7	41	♓	5	31
3	We.		2	4	14	7	42	♓	6	12
4	Th.	**CORPUS CHRISTI.**	2	4	14	7	43	♓	6	51
5	Fr.	summer weather.	2	4	13	7	44	♈	7	30
6	Sat.		1	4	13	7	45	♈	8	10
(23) 1st Sunday after Trinity. (Day's length, 15h. 33m.) ♃ in ♋										
7	Su.		1	4	12	7	45	♉	8	53
8	Mo.	**Henry G. Vennor died, 1884.**	1	4	12	7	46	♉	9	39
9	Tu.	Fair and warm—High winds and heavy	1	4	12	7	46	♉	10	28
10	We.	rains—Cool—Windy, warmer—Cool to	1	4	11	7	47	♊	11	21
11	Th.	**ST. BARNABAS.**	0	4	11	7	47	♊	Eve.	
12	Fr.	pleasant—Stormy—Frosts probable.	0	4	11	7	48	♋	1	14
13	Sat.		slo'	4	11	7	48	♋	2	11
(24) 2nd Sunday after Trinity. (Day's length, 15h. 38m.) ♄ in ♎										
14	Su.		0	4	11	7	49	♌	3	05
15	Mo.	Showers, with strong, high winds—	0	4	11	7	49	♌	3	56
16	Tu.		1	4	11	7	50	♍	4	45
17	We.	Changing to hot and sultry.	1	4	11	7	50	♍	5	33
18	Th.		1	4	11	7	51	♎	6	21
19	Fr.		1	4	11	7	51	♎	7	10
20	Sat.	**Accession Queen Victoria.**	1	4	11	7	51	♎	8	02
(25) 3rd Sunday after Trinity. (Day's length, 15h. 40m.) ♅ in ♎										
21	Su.		2	4	11	7	51	♏	8	57
22	Mo.	Opens rainy, cloudy, dull and very	2	4	12	7	52	♏	9	56
23	Tu.		2	4	12	7	52	♐	10	57
24	We.	**ST. JOHN BAPTIST.**—Mid-	2	4	12	7	52	♐	11	58
25	Th.	summer Day.	3	4	13	7	52	♑	Morn	
26	Fr.	unsettled—Finer, pleasant.	3	4	13	7	52	♑	0	57
27	Sat.		3	4	14	7	52	♒	1	51
(26) 4th Sunday after Trinity. (Day's length, 15h. 38m.) ♆ in ♉										
28	Su.		3	4	14	7	52	♒	2	40
29	Mo.	**ST. PETER and ST. PAUL.**	3	4	15	7	52	♓	3	25
30	Tu.	Fine, warm, summer weather.	4	4	15	7	51	♓	4	07

In this month the Mornings decrease 1 min. and the Afternoons increase 11 min.

PLANETS IN JUNE, 1896.

MONTREAL MEAN TIME.

ON MERIDIAN (SOUTH).	June 1st.	June 8th.	June 16th.	June 24th.
Mercury ...... ☿	0 51 ev.	0 12 ev.	11 24 mo.	10 48 mo.
Venus .... ♀	11 14 mo.	11 23 mo.	11 33 mo.	11 44 mo.
Mars .... ♂	7 52 mo.	7 42 mo.	7 32 mo.	7 22 mo.
Jupiter .... ♃	3 50 ev.	3 27 ev.	3 02 ev.	2 36 ev.
Saturn .... ♄	10 04 ev.	9 35 ev.	9 02 ev.	8 29 ev.
Uranus .... ♅	10 33 ev.	10 04 ev.	9 31 ev.	8 59 ev.
Neptune ...... ♆	0 25 ev.	10 58 mo.	11 28 mo.	10 57 mo.

THE PLANETS.—MERCURY plays a prominent part this month. He makes his Aphelion passage (farthest from the Sun) on the 8th at 6h. ev. ; two days later, at 8h. mo , he reaches Inferior Conjunction, passing between Earth and Sun and becoming a "Morning Star"; he is in Conjunction with Neptune on the 14th at 7h. ev., and 3° 57' S. of Venus on the 15th at 2h. 18m. mo. Reaching a "Stationary" position on the 22nd at 5h. mo.; he is for the second time during the month, in Conjunction with Neptune, passing his far away brother at 2h. mo. on the 30th (Neptune 2° 20' N.) VENUS is 1° 12' N. of Neptune on the 15th at 5h. mo. MARS is in Perihelion (nearest the Sun) on the 12th at 11h. mo.

THE MOON.—Will be 5° 48' N. of Mars on the 5th at 4h. 42m. ev. ; 5° 14' N. of Venus on the 10th at 1h. 15m ev. ; 6° 5' N. of Neptune the same day at 11h. 15m. ev.; 8° 3' N. of Mercury on the 11th at 2h. 45m. mo., 1° N. of Jupiter on the 14th at 4h. 17m. ev. ; 7° 49' S. of Saturn on the 21st at 2h. 43m. ev , and 5° 34' S. of Uranus on the 22nd at 2h. 49m. mo.

APOGEE: 5th, 3h. 45m. mo.; PERIGEE: 20th, 10h. 30m. mo.

THE STARS.—Lepus, "the Wolf," is a little Constellation below Orion, so near the horizon that it can only be well seen when it is on the meridian. It contains twenty-four Stars, including three of the third magnitude. The most favorable time for observation is about the end of June. Beta Lupi is a double Star, R.A. 5h. 23m., Dec. 20° 51' S. Its components are of the $3\frac{1}{2}$ and 11th magnitudes (deep yellow and blue). A most rapid binary system, or else, as Flammarion has suggested, a Sun and Planet.

7th Month, 1896.
31 Days.

JULY.

☉ enters ♌
22d. 4h. mo

Moon's Phases	Day.	BOSTON.	MONTREAL.	WASHINGTON	CHICAGO.	WINNIPEG.
☾ L.Q.	2	8.42 ev.	8.28 ev.	8.15 ev.	7.33 ev.	6.55 ev.
● N.M.	10	2.54 ev.	2.40 ev.	2.27 ev.	1.45 ev.	1.07 ev.
☽ F.Q.	17	11.23 mo.	11.09 mo.	10.56 mo.	10.14 mo.	9.36 mo.
☺ F.M.	24	1.04 ev.	0.50 ev.	0.37 ev.	11.55 mo.	11.17 mo.

DAYS. M.	DAYS. W.	WEATHER FORECAST.	MONTREAL. THE SUN Slow. M.	THE SUN Rises. H. M.	THE SUN Sets. H. M.	THE MOON Zod.	THE MOON Souths. H. M.
1	We.	**DOMINION DAY.**	4	4 16	7 51	♓	Morn
2	Th.	Fine, warm to hot summer weather,	4	4 16	7 51	♈	5 26
3	Fr.	with thunderstorms.	4	4 17	7 51	♈	6 06
4	Sat.	**INDEPENDENCE DAY.**	4	4 17	7 50	♈	6 47
(27) 5th Sunday after Trinity.		(Day's length, 15h. 32m.) ☿ in ♉					
5	Su.		4	4 18	7 50	♉	7 31
6	Mo.	Warm, sultry, heated term, with thun-	5	4 18	7 49	♉	8 19
7	Tu.		5	4 19	7 49	♊	9 11
8	We.	der—Fine and pleasant—Cool showers—	5	4 19	7 48	♊	10 06
9	Th.		5	4 20	7 48	♋	11 03
10	Fr.	Cloudy and squally—Showery at end.	5	4 21	7 47	♋	Eve.
11	Sat.		5	4 22	7 47	♌	0 57
(28) 6th Sunday after Trinity.		(Day's length, 15h. 23m.) ♀ in □					
12	Su.	Showery, cool—Fair and warm, with	5	4 23	7 46	♌	1 51
13	Mo.	variable winds.	6	4 24	7 46	♍	2 42
14	Tu.		6	4 25	7 45	♍	3 31
15	We.	**ST. SWITHIN.**	6	4 26	7 44	♍	4 19
16	Th.	Unsettled, threatening and cool at end	6	4 27	7 43	♎	5 07
17	Fr.	of week.	6	4 28	7 42	♎	5 58
18	Sat.		6	4 29	7 41	♏	6 51
(29) 7th Sunday after Trinity.		(Day's length, 15h. 10m.) ♂ in ♈					
19	Su.	Rainy, dull—Cloudy and unpleasant,	6	4 30	7 40	♏	7 48
20	Mo.		6	4 31	7 39	♐	8 47
21	Tu.	with changeful winds—Fine, warm sum-	6	4 32	7 38	♐	9 47
22	We.	mer weather at close of week.	6	4 33	7 37	♑	10 46
23	Th.		6	4 34	7 36	♑	11 41
24	Fr.	**Canada visited by Cartier, 1534.**	6	4 35	7 35	♒	Morn
25	Sat.	**ST. JAMES.**	6	4 36	7 34	♒	0 32
(30) 8th Sunday after Trinity.		(Day's length, 14h. 56m.) ♃ in ♌					
26	Su.		6	4 37	7 33	♒	1 18
27	Mo.	Opens dark and dull—A change to hot,	6	4 38	7 32	♓	2 02
28	Tu.		6	4 39	7 31	♓	2 42
29	We.	sultry, smoky, spell, with damaging thun-	6	4 40	7 30	♈	3 22
30	Th.	derstorms—Sultry and close.	6	4 41	7 29	♈	4 02
31	Fr.		6	4 42	7 28	♈	4 42

In this month the Mornings decrease 26 min. and the Afternoons 23 min. ☾

PLANETS IN JULY, 1896.

MONTREAL MEAN TIME.

ON MERIDIAN (SOUTH.)	July 1st.	July 8th.	July 16th.	July 24th.
Mercury .... ☿	10 34 mo.	10 36 mo.	10 57 mo.	11 33 mo.
Venus ...... ♀	11 54 mo.	0 04 ev.	0 15 ev.	0 25 ev.
Mars .... ♂	7 13 mo.	7 04 mo.	6 54 mo.	6 44 mo.
Jupiter ..... ♃	2 15 ev.	1 53 ev.	1 28 ev.	1 03 ev.
Saturn ...... ♄	8 01 ev.	7 33 ev.	7 01 ev.	6 30 ev.
Uranus .... ♅	8 31 ev.	8 03 ev.	7 31 ev.	6 59 ev.
Neptune .... ♆	10 31 mo.	10 05 mo.	9 34 mo.	9 04 mo.

THE PLANETS.—MERCURY is at Greatest Elongation West of the Sun of 21° 25' on the 3rd at 11h. ev. (visible before sunrise in the Eastern sky); on the 13th at 5h. ev. he is but 7' S of the Star *Mu Geminorum;* in Perihelion on the the 22nd at 5h. ev., he is in perfect Conjunction with the Star *Eta Cancri* on the 29th at 4h. mo., and reaches Superior Conjunction (passing behind the Sun) at 1h. ev. on the 31st. VENUS makes her passage behind the Sun (Superior Conjunction) on the 9th at 8h. mo., when she becomes an "Evening Star" for the rest of the year. She is in Perihelion on the 23rd at 4h. mo. SATURN is Stationary on the 16th at 11h. mo. URANUS Stationary on the 28th at 11h. ev.

THE MOON.—Near Mars on the 4th at 7h. 03m. ev.; will pass Neptune on the 8th at 9h. 13m. mo.; leave Mercury behind on the 9th at 11h. 30m. ev.; pass 2° 17' N. of Venus on the 10th at 2h. 41m. ev.; in close Conjunction with Jupiter (22' N.) on the 12th at 9h. 01m. mo.; be 7° 50' S. of Saturn on the 18th at 7h. 56m. ev.; and 5° 42' S. of Uranus on the 19th at 8h. 12m. mo.

APOGEE: 2nd, 10h. 20m. ev.; PERIGEE: 15th, 1h. ev.; APOGEE: 30th, 4h. 55m. ev.

THE STARS.—A compressed Mass of very small stars will be found in the Constellation *Scorpio,* in R.A. 16h. 16m., Dec. 26° 14' S. The cluster is large, rather dim, but resolvable into star points, and is followed by a vacant space devoid of Stars. The object is elongated and rather bright in its centre, has outlayers and a few stellar companions in the field of view. It is one and a half degrees West of the well known first magnitude Star *Antares.*

8th Month, 1896.
31 Days.

AUGUST.

☉ enters ♍
22d 0h. ev.

Moon's Phases	Day.	BOSTON.	MONTREAL.	WASHINGTON	CHICAGO.	WINNIPEG.
☾ L.Q.	1	1.53 ev.	1.39 ev.	1.26 ev.	0.44 ev.	0.06 ev.
● N.M.	8-9	0.21 mo.	0.07 mo.	11.54 ev.	11.12 ev.	10.34 ev.
☽ F.Q.	15	4.21 ev.	4.07 ev.	3.54 ev.	3.12 ev.	2.34 ev.
○ F.M.	23	2.23 mo.	2.09 mo.	1.56 mo.	1.14 mo.	0.36 mo.
☾ L Q.	31	6.14 mo.	6.00 mo.	5.47 mo.	5.05 mo.	4.27 mo.

DAYS. M.	DAYS. W.	WEATHER FORECAST.	MONTREAL. THE SUN Slow. M.	THE SUN Rises. H. M.	THE SUN Sets. H. M.	THE MOON Zod	THE MOON Souths. H. M.
1	Sat.	**LAMMAS DAY.**	6	4 43	7 27	♉	Morn
(31) 9th Sunday after Trinity. (Day's length, 14h. 41m.) ♄ in ♎							
2	Su.		6	4 45	7 26	♉	6 11
3	Mo.	Variable—Fair, warm and hot, with thun-	6	4 46	7 25	♊	7 00
4	Tu.		6	4 47	7 24	♊	7 53
5	We.	der and rain—Cooler, showery weather—	6	4 48	7 23	♊	8 49
6	Th.		6	4 50	7 21	♋	9 47
7	Fr.	Cloudy and rainy.	5	4 51	7 19	♋	10 44
8	Sat.		5	4 52	7 18	♌	11 39
(32) 10th Sunday after Trinity. (Day's length, 14h. 23m.) ☿ in ♌							
9	Su.	Fine, warm and pleasant, with local	5	4 53	7 16	♌	Eve.
10	Mo.	**ST. LAWRENCE.**	5	4 54	7 14	♍	1 23
11	Tu.	thunderstorms—Variable and rainy—Sud-	5	4 56	7 13	♍	2 13
12	We.	den squalls and rapid changes of tem-	5	4 57	7 11	♎	3 03
13	Th.		5	4 58	7 09	♎	3 54
14	Fr.	perature.	4	4 59	7 08	♏	4 47
15	Sat.	**ASSUMPTION B.V.M.**	4	4 00	7 07	♏	5 43
(33) 11th Sunday after Trinity. (Day's length, 14h. 04m.) ♀ in ♌							
16	Su.		4	5 02	7 06	♐	6 41
17	Mo.	Fine, clear and warm—A week of pleas-	4	5 03	7 04	♐	7 41
18	Tu.		3	5 04	7 02	♑	8 39
19	We.	ant, warm to hot summer weather, with	3	5 05	7 00	♑	9 35
20	Th.		3	5 06	6 58	♒	10 26
21	Fr.	indications of change at end of week.	3	5 08	6 56	♒	11 14
22	Sat.		3	5 09	6 54	♒	11 58
(34) 12th Sunday after Trinity. (Day's length, 13h. 42m.) ♂ in ♉							
23	Su.		2	5 10	6 52	♓	Morn
24	Mo.	**ST. BARTHOLOMEW.**	2	5 11	6 51	♓	0 39
25	Tu.	Unsettled, variable—Rains probable—	2	5 12	6 49	♓	1 19
26	We.		1	5 14	6 48	♈	1 59
27	Th.	Mild, pleasant weather, with gusty winds	1	5 15	6 46	♈	2 39
28	Fr.	—Warm to cool.	1	5 16	6 44	♉	3 20
29	Sat.		1	5 17	6 42	♉	4 05
(35) 13th Sunday after Trinity. (Day's length, 13h. 23m.) ♃ in ♌							
30	Su.	Fine and clear—Pleasant—Changeful	0	5 18	6 41	♉	4 52
31	Mo.	winds.	0	5 20	6 40	♊	5 42

In this month the Mornings decrease 37 min. and the Afternoons 47 min.

PLANETS IN AUGUST, 1896.

MONTREAL MEAN TIME.

ON MERIDIAN (SOUTH).	Aug. 1st.	Aug. 8th.	Aug. 16th.	Aug. 24th.
Mercury ☿	0 12 ev.	0 40 ev.	1 03 ev.	1 18 ev.
Venus ♀	0 33 ev.	0 40 ev.	0 46 ev.	0 52 ev.
Mars ♂	6 33 mo.	6 23 mo.	6 12 mo.	5 59 mo.
Jupiter ♃	0 39 ev.	0 17 ev.	11 53 mo.	11 28 mo.
Saturn ♄	6 00 ev.	5 33 ev.	5 03 ev.	4 34 ev.
Uranus ♅	6 27 ev.	6 02 ev.	5 30 ev.	5 15 ev.
Neptune ♆	8 33 mo.	8 06 mo.	7 36 mo.	7 04 mo.

THE PLANETS.—MERCURY is 1° 16′ N. of Jupiter on the 5th at 1h. mo., and on the 8th at 9h. mo. the little planet is only 18′ N. of Venus. VENUS and Jupiter are in close Conjunction (Venus 41′ N.) on the 2nd at 6h. ev. JUPITER is in Conjunction with the Sun on the 12th at 3h. mo., when he becomes a "Morning Star" for the rest of the year. SATURN reaches "Quadrature" (90° from the Sun) when he is overhead at 6h. ev., on the 4th at noon. URANUS is in a similar position on the 12th at 3h. ev.

THE MOON.—Is 7° N. of Mars on the 2nd at 4h. 44m. ev.; near Neptune on the 4th at 7h. 45m. ev.; only 16′ S. of Jupiter on the 9th at 4h. mo.; 1° 45′ S. of Venus the same day at 4h. 41m. ev.; in Conjunction with Mercury 1½ hours later; 7° 47′ S. of Saturn on the 15th at 2h. 34m. mo.; 5° 45′ S. of Uranus the same day at 1h. 48m. ev., and near Mars, for the second time this month, on the 31st at 8h. 41m. mo.

PERIGEE: 11th, 1h. 25m. ev.; ECLIPSED: 22nd-23rd [see page 17]; APOGEE: 27th, 9h. 35m. mo.

THE STARS.—The Star Gamma in Aquila (Tarazed) is a very fine double, carrying through space a very minute companion of the twelfth magnitude. In the field of the telescope is a curious double-curved row of Stars to the South. Gamma, in this Constellation, is now brighter than Beta, which may imply a change in one or both of these Stars, although in many instances, Bayer, who affixed the Greek letters in 1603, was not apparently entirely influenced by magnitude. R.A. of Tarazed 19h. 41m., Dec. 10° 19′ N.

9th Month, 1896.
30 Days.
SEPTEMBER.
⊙ enters ♎
22d. 8h. mo.

Moon's Phases	Day	BOSTON.	MONTREAL.	WASHINGTON	CHICAGO.	WINNIPEG.
● N.M.	7	9.02 mo.	8.48 mo.	8.35 mo.	7.53 mo.	7.15 mo.
☽ F.Q.	13	11.28 ev.	11.14 ev.	11.01 ev.	10.19 ev.	9.41 ev.
☺ F.M.	21	6.08 ev.	5.54 ev.	5.41 ev.	4.59 ev.	4.21 ev.
☾ L.Q.	29	9.17 ev.	9.03 ev.	8.50 ev.	8.08 ev.	7.30 ev.

DAYS.		WEATHER FORECAST.	MONTREAL.			
M.	W.		THE SUN Fast. Rises. Sets.			THE MOON Zod. Souths.
			M.	H. M.	H. M.	H. M.
1	Tu.		0	5 21	6 39	♊ Morn
2	We.	Bright, dry and windy—Mild, pleasant	1	5 22	6 37	♋ 7 32
3	Th.		1	5 23	6 35	♋ 8 28
4	Fr.	Cooler, with high winds and rain—Cloudy	1	5 24	6 33	♌ 9 24
5	Sat		2	5 26	6 31	♌ 10 18

(36) 14th Sunday after Trinity. (Day's length, 13h. 02m.) ♄ in ♎

6	Su.		2	5 27	6 29	♍ 11 10
7	Mo.	**LABOR DAY.**	2	5 28	6 27	♍ Eve.
8	Tu.		3	5 29	6 25	♎ 0 52
9	We.	Clear and fine September weather—	3	5 30	6 23	♎ 1 45
10	Th.	Windy and cloudy—High winds and rain	3	5 32	6 22	♎ 2 39
11	Fr.	—Cooler (frosts in Summer frost sections).	4	5 33	6 20	♏ 3 36
12	Sat.		4	5 34	6 18	♏ 4 30

(37) 15th Sunday after Trinity. (Day's length, 12h. 41m.) ♅ in ♎

13	Su.		4	5 35	6 16	♐ 5 35
14	Mo.	Cool to cold term of pleasant weather—	5	5 36	6 14	♐ 6 34
15	Tu.		5	5 38	6 12	♑ 7 31
16	We.	Bright, clear—Excellent weather for exhi-	5	5 39	6 10	♑ 8 23
17	Th.		6	5 40	6 08	♒ 9 11
18	Fr.	bitions and Summer travelling.	6	5 41	6 06	♒ 9 56
19	Sat.		7	5 42	6 04	♓ 10 38

(38) 16th Sunday after Trinity. (Day's length, 12h. 18m.) ☿ in ♍

20	Su.		7	5 44	6 02	♓ 11 18
21	Mo.	**ST. MATTHEW.**	7	5 45	6 00	♓ 11 57
22	Tu.		8	5 46	5 58	♈ Morn
23	We.	Fine weather continues to about 21st—	8	5 47	5 56	♈ 0 37
24	Th.	Dull, but fair and warm—Misty, with rain	8	5 48	5 54	♈ 1 18
25	Fr.	and wind probable—Fair at end.	9	5 50	5 53	♉ 2 01
26	Sat.		9	5 51	5 51	♉ 2 47

(39) 17th Sunday after Trinity. (Day's length, 11h 57m.) ♀ in ♍

27	Su.	Month closes fair, with mild and gusty	9	5 52	5 49	♊ 3 36
28	Mo.	winds.	10	5 53	5 47	♊ 4 28
29	Tu.	**MICHAELMAS.**	10	5 55	5 45	♋ 5 21
30	Wo.		10	5 56	5 43	♋ 6 16

In this month the Mornings decrease 35 min. and the Afternoons 56 min.

PLANETS IN SEPTEMBER, 1896.

MONTREAL MEAN TIME.

ON MERIDIAN (SOUTH).	Sept. 1st.	Sept. 8th.	Sept. 16th.	Sept. 24th.
Mercury .... ☿	1 27 ev.	1 30 ev.	1 27 ev.	1 10 ev.
Venus ...... ♀	0 57 ev.	1 00 ev.	1 05 ev.	1 10 ev.
Mars .... ♂	5 47 mo.	5 35 mo.	5 20 mo.	5 03 mo.
Jupiter ..... ♃	11 03 mo.	10 42 mo.	10 17 mo.	9 51 mo.
Saturn ...... ♄	4 04 ev.	3 39 ev.	3 10 ev.	2 41 ev.
Uranus ..... ♅	4 32 ev.	4 02 ev.	3 31 ev.	3 01 ev.
Neptune .... ♆	6 33 mo.	6 06 mo.	5 34 mo.	5 03 mo.

THE PLANETS.—MERCURY is in Aphelion on the 4th at 5h. ev. ; at Greatest Elongation East of the Sun of 26° 43' (well seen for a few evenings in the West after sunset) on, the 13th at 5h. mo. ; in Conjunction 4° 38' S. of Venus on the 24th at 2h. ev., and Stationary on the 26th at 5h. mo. MARS reaches Quadrature (90° from the Sun) when he is overhead at 6h. mo., on the 1st at 1h. mo. ; and is only 51' N. of Neptune on the 24th at 1h. mo. JUPITER is in Close Conjunction with the first magnitude Star *Alpha Leonis* (*Regulus*) on the 19th at 11h. mo., when he is only 20' N. of that beautiful brilliant (best seen prior to sunrise on the morning of the 19th.) NEPTUNE is 90° from the Sun on the 12th at 9h. mo., when he is overhead at 6h. mo., and Stationary on the 22nd at 3h. ev.

THE MOON.—Passes 6° 9' N. of Neptune on the 1st at 5h. 25m. mo. ; is in Close Conjunction (55' S.) with Jupiter on, the 6th, at 0h. 52m. mo. ; reaches the place of Venus on the 8th at 4h. 51m. ev. ; passes 2° 5' S. of Mercury on the 9th at 7h. 08m. mo. ; is 7° 38' S. of Saturn, on the 11th at 0h. 16m. ev. ; passes 5° 41' S. of Uranus on the 11th at 9h. 29m. ev. ; is near Neptune on the 28th at 1h. 06 m. ev., and close to Mars the same evening at 4h. 32m.

PERIGEE : 8th, 3h. ev. ; APOGEE : 23rd, 9h. 55m. ev.

THE STARS.—*Alpha Capricorni* is a noble double Star, obvious to the unaided eye. R.A. 20h. 11m., Decl. 12° 55' S. One of the stars has a star of the sixteenth magnitude as its companion.

10th Month, 1896. 31 Days.	OCTOBER.	☉ enters ♏ 22d. 6h. ev.

Moon's Phases	Day.	BOSTON.	MONTREAL.	WASHINGTON	CHICAGO.	WINNIPEG.
● N. M.	6	5.37 ev.	5.23 ev.	5.10 ev.	4.28 ev.	3.50 ev.
☽ F. Q.	13	10.06 mo.	9.52 mo.	9.39 mo.	8.57 mo.	8 19 mo.
☺ F. M.	21	11.36 mo.	11.22 mo.	11.09 mo.	10.27 mo.	9.49 mo.
☾ L. Q.	29	10.39 mo.	10.25 mo.	10.12 mo.	9 30 mo.	8.52 mo.

DAYS.		WEATHER FORECAST.	MONTREAL.			
			THE SUN		THE MOON	
M.	W.		Fast.	Rises.	Sets.	Zod. Souths.
			M.	H. M.	H. M.	H. M.
1	Th.		11	5 57	5 41	♌ Morn
2	Fr.	Dull, cloudy and cool.	11	5 59	5 39	♌ 8 04
3	Sat.		11	6 00	5 37	♌ 8 55

(40) 18th Sunday after Trinity. (Day's length, 11h. 34m.) ♂ in ♉

4	Su.		12	6 01	5 35	♍ 9 46
5	Mo.	Gusty, cool, dry, with sharp night frosts	12	6 03	5 34	♍ 10 37
6	Tu.	—Cloudy, very unsettled spell—Rain or	12	6 04	5 32	♎ 11 29
7	We.		12	6 05	5 30	♎ Eve.
8	Th.	sleet probable.	13	6 06	5 28	♏ 1 21
9	Fr.	ST. DENIS.	13	6 08	5 26	♏ 2 21
10	Sat.		13	6 09	5 25	♐ 3 23

(41) 19th Sunday after Trinity. (Day's length, 11h. 12m.) ♃ in ♌

11	Su.		13	6 11	5 23	♐ 4 25
12	Mo.	Columbus discov'd America, 1492.	14	6 12	5 21	♑ 5 24
13	Tu.	Misty and blustery, with rain and high	14	6 13	5 19	♑ 6 19
14	We.		14	6 15	5 17	♒ 7 09
15	Th.	winds (rough weather on Lakes and At-	14	6 16	5 16	♒ 7 55
16	Fr.	lantic seaboard)—Cold, bleak and rainy.	15	6 18	5 14	♓ 8 37
17	Sat.		15	6 19	5 12	♓ 9 18

(42) 20th Sunday after Trinity. (Day's length, 10h. 50m.) ♄ in ♎

18	Su.	ST. LUKE.	15	6 20	5 10	♓ 9 57
19	Mo.		15	6 21	5 08	♈ 10 37
20	Tu.	Bleak, cold and stormy generally, with	15	6 23	5 07	♈ 11 17
21	We.	flurries of snow and sharp (killing) frosts	15	6 24	5 05	♈ Morn
22	Th.		16	6 25	5 03	♉ 0 00
23	Fr.	—Sleet or snow probable.	16	6 26	5 01	♉ 0 45
24	Sat.		16	6 28	5 00	♊ 1 33

(43) 21st Sunday after Trinity. (Day's length, 10h. 29m.) ☿ in ♍

25	Su.		16	6 29	4 58	♊ 2 23
26	Mo.	Fine, warm and pleasant—A spell of	16	6 31	4 57	♊ 3 16
27	Tu.		16	6 32	4 55	♋ 4 10
28	We.	mild, open weather, with variable winds,	16	6 33	4 53	♋ 5 03
29	Th.	but warm at close.	16	6 35	4 52	♌ 5 55
30	Fr.		16	6 36	4 50	♌ 6 45
31	Sat.	All Hallow's Eve.	16	6 38	4 49	♍ 7 34

In this month the Mornings decrease 41 min. and the Afternoons 52 min.

PLANETS IN OCTOBER, 1896.

MONTREAL MEAN TIME.

ON MERIDIAN (SOUTH).		Oct. 1st.	Oct. 8th.	Oct. 16th.	Oct. 24th.
Mercury	☿	0 37 ev.	11 45 mo.	10 53 mo.	10 38 mo.
Venus	♀	1 15 ev.	1 20 ev.	1 27 ev.	1 36 ev.
Mars	♂	4 48 mo.	4 30 mo.	4 07 mo.	3 42 mo.
Jupiter	♃	9 29 mo.	9 07 mo.	8 41 mo.	8 14 mo.
Saturn......	♄	2 17 ev.	1 52 ev.	1 24 ev.	0 56 ev.
Uranus	♅	2 36 ev.	2 10 ev.	1 40 ev.	1 11 ev.
Neptune....	♆	4 35 mo.	4 08 mo.	3 36 mo.	3 04 mo.

THE PLANETS.—MERCURY passes Inferior Conjunction with the Sun on the 8th at 4h. ev. ; is stationary on the 17th at 0h. mo. ; in Perihelion on the 18th at 5h. ev. ; and at Greatest Elongation W. of 18° 26' on the 24th at 7h. mo. ; when he is to be looked for in the East prior to Sunrise. VENUS is close to Saturn (2° 25' S.) on the 15th at 3h. ev. (visible after sunset) and closer still (43' S.) to Uranus on the 19th at 2h. mo.

THE MOON.—Is 1° 40' S. of Jupiter on the 3rd at 9h. 17m. ev. ; close to Mercury (2° 3' S.) on the 7th at 0h. 37m. ev. ; passes 5° 18' S. of Venus on the 8th at 1h. 09m. ev. ; is in Conjunction with Saturn on the 9th at 1h. 30m. mo. ; passes 5° 32' S. of Uranus the same morning at 8h. 18m. ; is 5° 51' N. of Neptune on the 25th at 6h. 36m. ev. ; reaches the place of Mars on the 26th at 11h. 33m. mo., and is near Jupiter (2° 25' S.) on the 31st. at 3h. 13m. ev.

PERIGEE : 7th, 0h. mo. ; APOGEE : 21st, 1h. mo.

THE STARS.—In *Aquarius*, (R.A., 20h. 58m. ; Decl. 11° 50' S.) is a beautiful planetary Nebula, very bright for an object of this nature ; pale blue in color, and more like a Planet than a Nebula. In fact, were it not for its pale blue tint, the object would be a miniature of Venus. The Earl of Rosse noticed a thin "ray" on each side. At first it was thought to be a heap of stars, but the spectroscope of Huggins reveals the fact that it is a mass of incandescent gas. The star *Zeta* (also in this constellation) is an easy double. It is a fine object, its stars are of the fourth magnitude in R.A. 22h. 23m., Decl. 0° 38' S. They revolve about each other in a probable period of 750 years.

11th Month, 1896.
30 Days.

NOVEMBER.

☉ enters ♐
21d. 3h. ev.

Moon's Phases	Day.	BOSTON.	MONTREAL.	WASHINGTON	CHICAGO.	WINNIPEG.
● N.M.	5	2.46 mo.	2.32 mo.	2.19 mo.	1.37 mo.	0.59 mo.
☽ F.Q.	11-12	0.59 mo.	0.45 mo.	0.32 mo.	11.50 ev.	11.12 ev.
☺ F.M.	20	5.44 mo.	5.30 mo.	5.17 mo.	4.35 mo.	3.57 mo.
☾ L.Q.	27	10.03 ev.	9.49 ev.	9.36 ev.	8.54 ev.	8.16 ev.

DAYS. M.	DAYS. W.	WEATHER FORECAST.	MONTREAL. THE SUN. Fast. M.	THE SUN. Rises. H. M.	THE SUN. Sets. H. M.	THE MOON. Zod.	THE MOON. Souths. H. M.
(44) 22nd Sunday after Trinity. (Day's length, 10h. 08m.) ♀ in ♍							
1	Su.	**ALL SAINTS.**	16	6 39	4 47	♍	Morn
2	Mo.		16	6 41	4 46	♎	9 13
3	Tu.	Enters fair and warm for season—	16	6 42	4 44	♎	10 05
4	We.		16	6 44	4 43	♏	11 01
5	Th.	Cloudy—Sudden squalls, with snow flur-	16	6 45	4 41	♏	Eve.
6	Fr.	ries in Northern sections.	16	6 47	4 40	♐	1 04
7	Sat.		16	6 48	4 39	♐	2 08
(45) 23rd Sunday after Trinity. (Day's length, 9h. 48m.) ♂ in ♊							
8	Su.	A change to colder weather—Rains East	16	6 50	4 38	♑	3 11
9	Mo.	**Prince of Wales born, 1841.**	16	6 51	4 37	♑	4 09
10	Tu.	and West—A general storm period, stormy	16	6 53	4 35	♒	5 03
11	We.	**MARTINMAS.**	16	6 54	4 34	♒	5 51
12	Th.	on Atlantic, Gulf of St. Lawrence and	16	6 55	4 33	♒	6 35
13	Fr.	Lakes—Snow.	15	6 57	4 31	♓	7 16
14	Sat.		15	6 58	4 30	♓	7 56
(46) 24th Sunday after Trinity. (Day's length, 9h. 28m.) ♃ in ♌							
15	Su.		15	7 00	4 29	♈	8 36
16	Mo.	Dark, cold, cloudy weather, with sudden	15	7 01	4 28	♈	9 16
17	Tu.		15	7 02	4 27	♈	9 58
18	We.	squalls of wind—Stormy in N. and N.W.	14	7 03	4 26	♉	10 42
19	Th.		14	7 04	4 25	♉	11 29
20	Fr.	sections, with snow—Rains S and S.W.	14	7 06	4 24	♉	Morn
21	Sat.		14	7 08	4 23	♊	0 19
(47) 25th Sunday after Trinity. (Day's length, 9h. 13m.) ♄ in ♎							
22	Su.		13	7 09	4 22	♊	1 12
23	Mo.	Continues stormy—Dark, dull, threat-	13	7 10	4 22	♋	2 06
24	Tu.		13	7 12	4 21	♋	2 59
25	We.	**ST. CATHERINE.**	13	7 13	4 21	♌	3 51
26	Th.	ening, cloudy weather, with snow flurries	12	7 14	4 20	♌	4 41
27	Fr.	in sections—Closes stormy.	12	7 15	4 20	♍	5 29
28	Sat.		12	7 16	4 19	♍	6 16
(48) 1st Sunday in Advent. (Day's length, 9h. 01m.) ♅ in ♎							
29	Su.	Continues stormy and windy, but	11	7 18	4 19	♍	7 04
30	Mo.	**ST. ANDREW.** warmer.	11	7 19	4 18	♎	7 53

In this month the Mornings decrease 40 min. and the Afternoons 29 min.

PLANETS IN NOVEMBER, 1896.

MONTREAL MEAN TIME.

ON MERIDIAN (SOUTH).	Nov. 1st.	Nov. 8th.	Nov. 16th.	Nov. 24th.
Mercury .... ☿	10 46 mo.	10 59 mo.	11 17 mo.	11 37 mo.
Venus ...... ♀	1 46 ev.	1 55 ev.	2 07 ev.	2 19 ev.
Mars .... ♂	3 13 mo.	2 44 mo.	2 07 mo.	1 27 mo.
Jupiter ..... ♃	7 47 mo.	7 23 mo.	6 55 mo.	6 27 mo.
Saturn ...... ♄	0 28 ev.	0 04 ev.	11 37 mo.	11 09 mo.
Uranus ..... ♅	0 41 ev.	0 15 ev.	11 45 mo.	11 16 mo.
Neptune .... ♆	2 32 mo.	2 04 mo.	1 31 mo.	0 59 mo.

THE PLANETS.—MERCURY and Saturn are in Conjunction (Saturn 1° 50′ N.) on the 19th at 3h. ev. ; the little Planet passing nearer still to Uranus (13′ S.) on the 21st at 0h. 13m. morn., and reaching Conjunction with the Sun (Superior) on the 28th at 1h. eve. VENUS is in Aphelion on the 12th at 11h mo. MARS is Stationary on the 2nd at 1h. mo. JUPITER is at Quadrature (90° from the Sun) and overhead at 6h. mo., on the 30th at 5h ev. SATURN reaches Conjunction with the Sun on the 13th at 9h. mo. URANUS reaches Conjunction with the Sun on the 16th at 10h. mo.

THE MOON.—Passes 6° 59′ S. of Mercury on the 4th at 6h. 50m. mo. ; is near Saturn on the 5th at 5h. 12m. ev. ; close to Uranus the same evening at 9h. 32m. ; is 5° 44′ N. of Neptune on the 21st at 11h 11m. ev. ; passes Mars on the 22nd at 0h. 01m. ev., and reaches the place of Jupiter on the 28th at 4h. 31m. mo.

PERIGEE : 4th, 11h. 50m. mo. ; APOGEE : 17th, 4h. 35m. mo.

THE STARS.—In Cepheus (R.A. 21h. 40m., Decl. 58° 14′ N.), is situated the celebrated "Garnet Sidus" of Herschell. A fine red star, it is visible to the unaided eye. It is a variable star, changing from the fourth to the sixth magnitude in five or six years. Herschel described it as of "a very fine deep garnet color." In R.A. 0h. 52m., Decl. 81° 14′ N. is a double star of the seventh magnitude, its Components bluish and ruddy, remarkable as the most rapid variable known, its increase, decrease and minima are each of two hours duration.

12th Month, 1896 31 Days.	DECEMBER.	⊙ enters ♑ 21d. 2h. mo.			

Moon's Phases	Day.	BOSTON.	MONTREAL.	WASHINGTON	CHICAGO.	WINNIPEG.
● N. M.	4	1.10 ev.	0.56 ev.	0.43 ev.	0.01 ev.	11.23 mo.
☽ F. Q.	11	7.48 ev.	7.34 ev.	7.21 ev.	6.39 ev.	6.01 ev.
☺ F. M.	19	11.24 ev.	11.10 ev.	10.57 ev.	10.15 ev.	9.37 ev.
☾ L. Q.	27	7.27 mo.	7.13 mo.	7.00 mo.	6.18 mo.	5.40 mo.

DAYS.		WEATHER FORECAST.	MONTREAL.			
M.	W.		THE SUN — Fast.	Rises.	Sets.	THE MOON Zod. Souths.
1	Tu.		10	7 20	4 18	♎ Morn
2	We.	High winds, rain (or snow)—Unsettled	10	7 21	4 18	♏ 9 41
3	Th.		10	7 22	4 17	♏ 10 41
4	Fr.	—Cold, windy, with snow.	9	7 23	4 16	♐ 11 45
5	Sat.		9	7 24	4 16	♐ Eve.

(49) 2nd Sunday in Advent. (Day's length, 8h. 49m.) ♆ in ♉

6	Su.		8	7 26	4 15	♑ 1 52
7	Mo.	Unsettled—Stormy downfall rain or	8	7 27	4 15	♑ 2 50
8	Tu.	**CONCEPTION B. V. M.**	8	7 28	4 14	♒ 3 42
9	We.		7	7 29	4 14	♒ 4 29
10	Th.	sleet, with drifts and bluster—windy, but	7	7 30	4 15	♓ 5 12
11	Fr.	clear and milder.	6	7 31	4 15	♓ 5 53
12	Sat.		6	7 33	4 15	♓ 6 33

(50) 3rd Sunday in Advent. (Day's length, 8h. 42m.) ☿ in ♐

13	Su.		5	7 34	4 16	♈ 7 13
14	Mo.		5	7 35	4 16	♈ 7 54
15	Tu.	Mild weather—Quite warm for season—	4	7 36	4 17	♉ 8 37
16	We.		4	7 37	4 17	♉ 9 24
17	Th.	Fine, clear, soft—A marked mild period.	3	7 38	4 18	♉ 10 13
18	Fr.		3	7 39	4 18	♊ 11 05
19	Sat.		2	7 40	4 19	♊ Morn

(51) 4th Sunday in Advent. (Day's length, 8h. 39m.) ♀ in ♑

20	Su.		2	7 40	4 19	♋ 0 01
21	Mo.	**ST. THOMAS.**	1	7 41	4 20	♋ 0 54
22	Tu.	Mild weather continues, with rains—	1	7 41	4 20	♌ 1 47
23	We.	Change to clear, cold and stormy spell—	0	7 42	4 21	♌ 2 38
24	Th.	Milder at end of week.	slo'	7 42	4 21	♍ 3 27
25	Fr.	**CHRISTMAS.**	1	7 43	4 22	♍ 4 14
26	Sat.	**ST. STEPHEN.**	1	7 43	4 23	♍ 5 01

(52) 1st Sunday after Christmas. (Day's length, 8h. 41m.) ♂ in ♉

27	Su.	**ST. JOHN EVANGELIST.**	2	7 43	4 24	♎ 5 48
28	Mo.	Colder—Sharper—High winds—Dull,	2	7 43	4 24	♎ 6 37
29	Tu.	cloudy and threatening.	3	7 42	4 25	♏ 7 30
30	We.	**Henry G. Vennor born, 1840.**	3	7 42	4 26	♏ 8 26
31	Th.		4	7 42	4 26	♐ 9 27

In this month the Mornings decrease 22 min. and the Afternoons increase 8 min.

PLANETS IN DECEMBER, 1896.

MONTREAL MEAN TIME.

ON MERIDIAN (SOUTH).	Dec. 1st.	Dec. 8th.	Dec. 16th.	Dec. 24th.
Mercury .... ☿	11 56 mo.	0 16 ev.	0 40 ev.	1 04 ev.
Venus ...... ♀	2 28 ev.	2 38 ev.	2 47 ev.	2 54 ev.
Mars .... ♂	0 49 mo.	0 09 mo.	11 19 ev.	10 36 ev.
Jupiter .... ♃	6 02 mo.	5 36 mo.	5 06 mo.	4 35 mo.
Saturn ..... ♄	10 45 mo.	10 20 mo.	9 53 mo.	9 25 mo.
Uranus .... ♅	10 50 mo.	10 25 mo.	9 55 mo.	9 25 mo.
Neptune .... ♆	0 31 mo.	0 02 mo.	11 30 ev.	10 53 ev.

THE PLANETS.—On the 1st at 4h. ev., MERCURY is in Aphelion (farthest from the Sun.). MARS on the 10th-11th at midnight, reaches Opposition to the Sun, when he is at greatest brilliancy and overhead at midnight. JUPITER is Stationary on the 25th at 8h. ev. SATURN and Uranus are in Conjunction (Saturn 1° 49' N.) on the 28th at 8h. mo. NEPTUNE, at 4h. mo. on the 10th is at Opposition, when he is overhead at midnight and in most favourable position for observation.

THE MOON.—Is 7° 11' S. of Saturn on the 3rd at 9h. 09m. mo.; passes 5° 21' S. of Uranus on the same day at 11h. 08m. mo.; is 3° 2' S. of Mercury on the 4th at 7h. 29m. ev.; very close to Venus (3' N.) on the 7th at 8h. 48m. mo.; approaches within 1° 35' of Mars on the 19th at 0h. 18m. mo.; is 5° 45' N. of Neptune four hours later; leaves Jupiter behind on the 25th at 0h. 23m. ev.; is 5° 25' S. of Uranus on the 30th at 10h. 41m. ev., and makes the final-Conjunction of the year with Saturn (passing 7° 15' S.) the same evening at 10h. 53m.

PERIGEE: 2nd, 9h. 25m. ev.; APOGEE: 14th, 7h. 05m. ev.; PERIGEE: 30th, 7h. 30m. ev.

THE STARS—The Star Gamma, in Aries (Mesartim) R.A. 1h. 47m., Decl. 18° 42' N., is an interesting object. Its Components are of the 4½ and 5th magnitude, bright white and pale grey respectively. It is a good object for a small telescope, and was discovered to be a double Star by Hooke when engaged following the Comet of 1664.

*SEED SOWING—1896.

LATITUDE 35°.

Favourable times for sowing and transplanting in Virginia, West Virginia, North and South Carolina, Georgia, Kentucky, Tennessee, Arkansas, Southern Missouri, Northern Texas, Arizona, Indian Territory, New Mexico, California, and all places in North America at or near Latitude 35° N.

JANUARY.—The 1st has ☽ in ♋ and ♓ rising from 10.10 to 11.20 morn.; and ♉ rising from 1.15 to 2.50 aft., which times are good for things which fruit below ground (roots). The 17th, 18th, and 19th will see ☽ in ♓, rising from 9.10 to 10.25 morn., good for roots and potatoes. The same days are good for all other things from 11.35 morn., to 1.00 aft., when ♉ rises. The 23rd and 24th have ☽ in ♉ and ♓ rising from 8.50 to 10.05 morn., and ♉ rising between 11.25 morn. and 12.50 aft., good for roots. The garden truck and all things which fruit above ground, including tomatoes, grain, vines, etc., 3.00 to 5.00 aft. (♋ rising). The 27th and 28th (☽ in ♋ and ♓ rising) from 8.15 to 9.30 morn.; and (♉ rising) 10.50 morn. to 12.15 noon., good for roots. All other things, between 2.15 and 4.25 aft. when ♋ rises.

FEBRUARY.—The 14th, 15th and 16th ☽ is in ♓ rising, from 7.15 to 8.30 morn.; ♉ rising, 9.50 to 11.10 morn., and, (♋ rising) from 1.10 to 3.20 aft., all which times are excellent for sowing and transplanting things which fruit above ground, grain, fruit, vines, Spring salads, etc. The 19th, 20th and 21st have ☽ in ♉ with ♓ rising from 6.50 to 8.00 morn., good for things of downward growth; also, (♉ rising) between 9.20 and 10.45 morn.; and (♋ rising) 12.25 noon to 2.35 aft., both times are good for grain, vines, etc. The 24th and 25th have ☽ in ♋ and ♉ rising from 6.25 to 7.40 morn., and (♉ rising) from 9.00 to 10.35 morn. These times are good for roots. The same afternoon from 12.20 to 2.30 are good for all other things when ♋ rises.

MARCH.—The 14th with ☽ in ♓ rising from 5.20 to 6.35 morn.; (♉ rising) 7.55 to 9.20 morn.; and (♋ rising) 11.20 morn. to 1.30 aft. is a good date for grain, vines, Spring salads, etc. The 18th and 19th are excellent days, when ☽ is in ♉ with ♓ rising from 5.00 to 6.10 morn., good for

* The local time, at the place mentioned, is meant in every case.

roots. For grain, vines, and all other things try (♉ rising)
7.35 to 9.00 morn., and (♋ rising) 11.15 morn., to 1.20 aft.
The 22nd and 23rd have ☽ in ♋ with ♓ rising from 4.50
to 6.00 morn., and (♉ rising) from 7.25 to 8.55 morn., good
for roots. All other things (corn, grain, vines, squash, etc.)
11.10 morn. to 1.15 aft., when ♋ rises. The 28th, 29th and
30th have ☽ in ♎ with ♉ rising from 6.55 to 8.20 morn.,
and (♋ rising) 10.20 morn., to 12.30 noon, all good for
roots; for grain, vines, squash, and similar things, 5.35 to
8.00 eve. (♎ rising.)

APRIL.—The 14th and 15th have ☽ in ♉ rising from
5.45 to 7.10 morn., (good for roots); (♋ rising) 9.15 to
11.25 morn ; and (♎ rising) 4.30 to 6.45 aft., are excellent
for sowing Spring wheat, corn, other grain, as well as vegetables, squash, cucumbers, etc. The 18th and 19th, when ☽
is in ♋ and ♋ rises from 9.00 to 11.10 morn.; also (♎
rising) from 4.15 to 6.35 aft., both excellent for Spring
wheat, corn, squash and all things which fruit above ground.
The 25th and 26th have ☽ in ♎ with ♉ rising from 5.00
to 6.25 morn., also (♋ rising) 8.40 to 10.50 morn., good for
roots. All other things, grain, vines, etc., from 4.00 to 6.20
aft., when ♎ rises with ☽ therein. An excellent time for
Spring wheat.

MAY.—The 16th and 17th are good when ☽ is in ♋
rising from 7.20 to 9.30 morn., and (♎ rising) from 2.20 to
4.40 aft. (excellent for grain, vines, flower seeds, etc.) The
22nd and 23rd are good, when ☽ is in ♎ and ♋ rises from
7.00 to 9.10 morn., (good for roots) and (♎ rising) from
2.00 to 4.20 aft., good for grain, vines, squash, flower seeds,
etc.

JUNE.—The 12th and 13th are good, when ☽ is in ♋
rising from 5.35 to 7.45 morn., also (♎ rising) from 12.50
noon, to 3.15 aft. These times are best for crops of upward
growth, such as grain, vines, etc. The ☽ is in ♎ on the
18th, 19th and 20th, and ♎ rises from 11.55 morn., to 2.10
aft., when all kinds of things which fruit above ground may
be sown, set or transplanted.

JULY.—The 16th and 17th, when ☽ is in ♎ rising are
good, from 10.05 morn to 12.30 noon.

AUGUST.—The 12th and 13th have ☽ in ♎ rising from
8.40 to 11.05 morn. The 23rd, 24th and 25th when ☽ is

‎

in ♓ and ♎ rising are also good dates from 8.00 to 10.25 morn.

SEPTEMBER.—The 8th, 9th and 10th are good, from 7.00 to 9.25 morn., when ☽ is in ♎ rising; also, from 5.40 to 6.55 aft. when ♓ rises. The latter excellent for grain sowing. The 19th, 20th and 21st have ☽ in ♓ and ♎ rising from 6.15 to 8.40 morn., and (♓ rising) from 5.00 to 6.15 aft. The latter especially for Fall grain.

OCTOBER.—The 7th when ☽ is in ♎ with ♓ rising from 3.45 to 5.00 aft. The 16th, 17th and 18th with ☽ in ♓ rising from 2.55 to 4.05 aft. are excellent for sowing grain.

NOVEMBER.—The 13th and 14th from 1.10 to 2.30 aft., when ☽ is in ♓ rising, are good for grain. Also the 18th, 19th and 20th from 12.55 to 2.05 aft., are good for grain, with ☽ in ♉ and ♓ rising.

DECEMBER.—The 10th, 11th and 12th are good from 11.15 morn. to 12.35 noon (☽ in ♓ rising.) Also the 15th, 16th and 17th from 11.05 morn. to 12.25 noon, (☽ in ♉ and ♓ rising.)

LATITUDE 40°.

Favorable times for sowing in Maryland, District of Columbia, Pennsylvania, Delaware, New Jersey, Southern New York, Rhode Island, Connecticut, Ohio, Indiana, Southern Illiniois, Northern Missouri, Iowa, Kansas, Nebraska, Utah Territory, Nevada, Colorado, and all places at or near Latitude 40° North. (For Moon's place in Zodiac at these times see Calendar pages or table for Latitude 35° N.)

MARCH.—The 14th, from 5.25 to 6.25 morn.; 7.55 to 9.15 morn, and 11.10 morn to 1.20 aft., is good for all kinds of grain, vines, Spring salads, flower seeds, etc. The 18th and 19th are excellent from 5.20 to 6.30 morn., good for roots. For grain, vines, and all other things, 7.45 to 9.05 morn., and 11.05 morn. to 1.15 aft. The 22nd and 23rd, from 5.00 to 6.00 morn., and 7.25 to 8.50 morn., good for roots. All other things, corn, grain, vines, squash, etc., 11.00 morn. to 1.05 aft. The 28th, 29th and 30th, from 7.00 to 8.20 morn., and 10.15 morn. to 12.20 noon, are good for roots; other things, 5.40 to 8.10 eve.

APRIL.—The 14th and 15th, from 5.40 to 7.00 morn., are good for roots; other things, 9.00 to 11.15 morn., and 4.30 to 6.50 aft. the latter especially for Spring wheat, corn, vegetables, squash, cucumbers, etc. The 18th and 19th, from 5.35 to 6.50 morn. ; also 8.50 to 11.05 morn., and 4.20 to 6.40 aft., excellent for Spring wheat, corn, squash, and all things which fruit above ground. The 25th and 26th, from 4.55 to 6.25 morn. ; also 8.30 to 10.45 morn., are good for roots. For all other things, grain, vines, etc., 3.55 to 6.15 aft. Excellent for Spring wheat.

MAY.—The 16th and 17th, from 7.00 to 8.00 morn., and 2.20 to 4.50 aft., are excellent for grain, vines, flower seeds, etc. The 22nd and 23rd, from 6.40 to 8.40 morn., are good for roots ; and all other things, grain, vines, squash, flower seeds, etc., from 2.00 to 4.25 aft.

JUNE.—The 12th and 13th, from 5.10 to 7.25 morn.; also from 12.30 noon to 3.05 aft. ; excellent for crops of upward fruiting, such as grain, vines, etc. The 18th 19th and 20th, from 4.50 morn. to 7.00 morn., and 12.10 noon to 2.40 aft., are good.

JULY.—The 16th and 17th are good from 10.30 morn. to 12.35 noon.

AUGUST.—The 12th and 13th, from 8.30 to 11.00 morn. The 23rd, 24th and 25th, from 7.55 to 10.25 morn.

SEPTEMBER.—The 8th, 9th and 10th, from 7.05 to 9.35 morn. ; also, from 5.45 to 6.55 aft. The latter especially for Fall grain. The 19th, 20th and 21st, from 6.10 to 8.35 morn., and 4.55 to 6.10 aft. The latter for grain.

OCTOBER.—The 7th, from 3.50 to 5.00 aft. Good for grain. The 16th, 17th and 18th, from 3.10 to 4.10 aft., are excellent for Fall grain.

LATITUDE 45°.

Favorable times for sowing in Massachusetts, New Hampshire, Vermont, Maine, Nova Scotia, New Brunswick, Prince Edward Island, Quebec, Ontario, Northern New York, Michigan, Northern Illinois, Wisconsin, Southern Minnesota, South Dakota, Southern Idaho, Wyoming, Southern Montana, Oregon, Southern Washington Territory, and all places in North America at or near Lat. 45° N. (For Moon's place in Zodiac at these times, see Calendar pages, or table for Lat. 35° N.)

MARCH.—(*Calculated especially for greenhouse and framework.*) The 14th, from 5.40 to 6.55 morn. ; 8.05 to 9.20

morn., and 11.10 morn to 1.20 aft. The 18th and 19th, from 7.50 to 9.15 morn.; and 11.35 to 1.40 aft. The 22nd and 23rd, from 7.40 to 9.05 morn.; 11.25 morn. to 1.30 aft., and 6.25 to 8.40 eve. The 28th, 29th and 30th, from 6.25 to 7.35 morn.; 9.35 to 11.05 morn., and 5.25 to 8.00 eve.

APRIL.—The 14th and 15th, from 5.55 to 7.10 morn., are good for roots; other things, 9.05 to 11.20 morn., and 4.45 to 7.20 aft., the latter especially for corn, Spring wheat, vegetables, squash, cucumbers, flower seeds, etc. The 18th and 19th, from 5.35 to 6.45 morn.; also, 8.55 to 11.00 morn., and 4.25 to 7.05 aft. Excellent for Spring wheat, corn, squash, etc. The 25th. and 26th from 5.00 to 6.10 morn., also, 8.10 to 10.25 morn., are good for roots, potatoes, etc. All other things, grain, vines, etc., 3.50 to 6.25 aft. Very good for Spring wheat.

MAY.—The 16th and 17th, from 6.50 to 9.05 morn., and 2.30 to 5.10 aft., are excellent for grain, vines, flower seeds, etc. The 22nd and 23rd, from 6.15 to 8.45 morn., are good for roots; and all other things, (grain vines, squash, flower seed, etc.) from 2.00 to 4.30 aft.

JUNE.—The 12th and 13th, from 5.05 to 7.20 morn., also from 12.30 noon to 2.55 aft.; excellent for crops of upward growth, such as grain, corn, vines, etc. The 18th, 19th and 20th, from 4.40 to 6.50 morn., and 12.00 noon to 2.35 aft., are also good.

JULY.—The 16th and 17th, from 10.30 noon to 1.20 aft.

AUGUST.—The 12th and 13th, from 8.40 to 11.15 morn. The 23rd, 24th and 25th, from 7.50 to 10.25 morn.

SEPTEMBER.—The 8th, 9th and 10th, from 7.00 to 9.40 morn.; also from 6.00 to 7.00 aft. The latter especially for Fall grain. The 19th, 20th and 21st, from 6.10 to 8.45 morn, and 5.10 to 6.10 aft. The latter is best for Fall grain.

OCTOBER.—The 7th, from 4.15 to 5.15 aft. Good for grain. The 16th, 17th and 18th, from 3.20 to 4.20 aft., are excellent for Fall grain.

LATITUDE 50°.

Favorable times for sowing in Newfoundland, Manitoba, North-West Territories, North Dakota, Northern Montana, Northern Minnesota, Northern Washington Territory, Northern Idaho, British Columbia, and all places in North

America, at or near Latitude 50° North. (For Moon's place in Zodiac at these times, see Calendar pages, or table for Lat. 35° N.) .

APRIL.—The 14th and 15th, from 5.35 to 6.40 morn., are good for roots; other things, 8.40 to 10.55 morn., and 4.30 to 7.10 aft., the latter especially for Spring wheat, corn, vegetables, cucumbers, squash, flower seeds, etc. The 18th and 19th, from 5.10 to 6.15 morn.; also 7.55 to 10.15 morn., and 4.15 to 6.55 aft., are excellent for Spring wheat, corn, squash, etc. The 25th and 26th, from 4.55 to 6.00 morn.; also 8.05 to 10.25 morn., are good for roots, potatoes, etc. All other things, grain, vines, etc., 3.40 to 6.15 aft. Very good, especially for wheat.

MAY.—The 16th and 17th, from 6.30 to 8.45 morn., and 2.30 to 5.20 aft., are excellent for grain, vines, flower seed, etc. The 22nd and 23rd, from 5.55 to 8.30 morn., are good for roots, and for all other things, (grain, vines, squash, flower seeds, etc.,) from 2.00 to 4.50 aft.

JUNE.—The 12th and 13th, from 4.45 to 7.00 morn.; also, from 12.45 noon to 3.35 aft., excellent for crops of upward growth (grain, vines, corn, squash, etc.). The 18th, 19th and 20th, from 4.00 to 6.30 morn., and 12.00 noon to 2.50 aft., are also good.

JULY.—The 16th and 17th, from 10.25 morn. to 1.15 aft.

AUGUST.—The 12th and 13th, from 8.30 to 11.10 morn. The 23rd, 24th and 25th, from 7.50 to 10.40 morn.

SEPTEMBER.—The 8th, 9th and 10th, from 7.00 to 9.50 morn.; also from 6.00 to 6.50 aft. The latter for Fall grain. The 19th, 20th and 21st, from 6.10 to 9.00 morn., and 5.20 to 6.10 aft. The latter for Fall grain.

OCTOBER.—The 7th, from 4.00 to 4.50 aft. The 16th, 17th and 18th, from 3.30 to 4.20 aft. Excellent for Fall grain.

Quick germination is the first thing needful, the critical time of every known seed being the first few days after fructification. Put in wheat with Virgo rising and a poor crop is generally the result, no seed, and scarcely any straw.

THE AURORA BOREALIS.

H. B. SMALL.

So little is generally known about the Aurora Borealis, or "Northern Lights," that a short article descriptive of this meteorological phenomenon may prove interesting to our readers. For a number of years past, Dr. M. A. Veeder, of Lyons, N.Y., has made a specialty of collecting and tabulating records of observations of the Aurora from all parts of the globe, to be used in comparison with those taken by Lieut. Peary, and other Arctic Explorers in Greenland and around the magnetic pole near Hudson Bay. Mr. H. B. Small, of Ottawa, is his Canadian observer, and he has furnished records of his observations of the occurrence of the phenomenon for the last two years. Dr. Veeder has by this means substantiated the theory that storms of a magnetic nature can be predicted with accuracy in advance of their occurrence.

Auroras may be demonstrated to be the immediate effect of violent disturbances on the Sun's surface, due to currents of positive electricity illuminating the atmosphere in their passage to the earth, and are as peculiar to the polar, as thunderstorms are to the tropical areas. With an increase of the Sun heat, whether diurnal or annual, the auroral Zone moves towards the Equator and with an increase of cold travels poleward. When the solar temperature is increased, the supply of atmospheric electricity is increased proportionately, and thus the Aurora is a valuable index of well marked though not immediate, meteorological changes. Just how the solar disturbance which causes the terrestrial phenomenon of an Aurora originates the atmospheric disturbance has never been fully explained. But it is clear if the original solar disturbance occasions a decided cyclone in our atmosphere, a large anticyclone will attend the storm, for the latter is mechanically impossible without the former, and the anticyclone invariably gives rise, except in summer, to more or less severe cold.

Now Auroras and magnetic storms increase and diminish in like ratio with each other and in proportion to Sun spots. But something else besides spots help to produce these magnetic phenomena, and these are Eruptions of glowing vapor known as "Faculæ." In 1859 an outbreak of Faculæ was coincident with a violent magnetic storm and Aurora, but with the exception of one other similar occurrence referred to by Prof. C. A. Young in his "Treatise on the Sun," nothing having sufficient precision to be worthy of notice has been published. But the occasional outbreak of an Aurora or a magnetic storm at times when there are no dark spots on the sun, is traceable to "Faculæ." The finest Auroras of recent years have appeared 26 or 27 days apart, such recurrence closely approximating the time of the revolution of the Sun, and the point most powerful in influencing the display is on the Sun's eastern limb. Observations have now given evidence that solar disturbances originate Auroras when by rotation they appear at the Sun's eastern edge. Dr. Veeder says that out of 188 well defined outbreaks of Aurora in three years, 162 of these by actual observation disclosed a disturbance on the Sun's eastern edge. When no auroras were visible within the borders of the United States, although the outbreaks on the Sun were noticed, there was a manifest increase in thunderstorms, as though they had taken the place of Aurora. Observations now show that on the days when solar disturbances are in process of being directed earthwards, either by the rotation of the Sun on its axis, or by some sudden outbreak of the eruptive forces, there is an immediate impulse given to the atmosphere and perhaps even to the solid portions of the earth itself. Years ago Dr. Veeder began to seek to identify the precise solar conditions on which the Aurora depends, and why the Aurora remains visible for one or two nights only, although the disturbance that is presumed to originate it remains in most cases on the earthward side of the Sun for nearly a fortnight. He now thinks this is due in part to difference of character of the eruptions on the Sun and in part to difference in terrestrial conditions. Grouping together phenomena as they appear from day to day makes it probable there are several terrestrial conditions which are more or less related to each other and to certain solar conditions. For instance, on certain days on which they are in progress barometric depressions are deepened, the crests of anticyclones heightened, the gradients of temperature and atmospheric pressure becoming steeper, the winds stronger, the rainfalls greater, thunderstorms more severe, and their place in winter supplied by blizzards. In this connection the attention of observers should be called to noticing and to recording the existence of a secondary diurnal maximum of the thunderstorms between midnight and morning, the colors of the lightning flashes which have been found to range from steel blue to cherry red. Also any persistence of phosphorescence or lurid appearance of the sky between successive flashes; also the exact time of any sudden notable increase in thunderstorm action. At times thunderstorms suddenly become much more energetic over wide areas as far as can be determined at the same instant of time, thus corresponding precisely to a similar behaviour of the Aurora.

If the eruptions on the Sun are of such a character as to give origin to metallic vapors as shown by the spectroscope, an Aurora is a certain accompaniment, and in such cases disturbances of the Earth currents, known as magnetic storms, occur, and even the solid crust of the earth itself receives impulses that cause tremors and that may precipitate genuine earthquake shocks in localities where the conditions are favorable because of instability existing therein.

The results gained by observation at various places, by the daily weather charts covering nearly the entire northern hemisphere, and telegraphic information in regard to the more remarkable displays are now making it more possible to trace out with some degree of certainty the relations borne by the Sun in regard to these phenomena. Nothing of a satisfactory nature to account for the Aurora previously was obtainable, and those who after reading this article may witness an unusually bright display, may rest assured that scientific observers are recording any remarkable features in the same, and that simultaneous record is being made in various quarters of the globe, for comparison and reference.

FOR SALE.

SMITH'S PLANETARY ALMANAC,

WITH

ASTRONOMICAL LIBRARY,

AND

Weather Notes for each Day for Past Years.

The Almanac has been before the public Nineteen Years,
and circulates throughout the United States and Canada.

For Particulars, apply to

MRS. W. H. SMITH,

215 PINE AVENUE,

MONTREAL, Can.

SEE LIST OF BACK NUMBERS

OF

SMITH'S PLANETARY ALMANAC,

Advertised in this Issue.

These Early Numbers will be valuable in a few years.

PRICE, TEN CENTS EACH.

For Sale only by Publisher,

215 PINE AVENUE,

MONTREAL, CANADA,

ST. LAWRENCE HALL

MONTREAL, P.Q.

For upwards of thirty-five years the name of the **St. Lawrence Hall** *has been familiar to all travellers on this Continent. The Hotel is* **CONVENIENTLY SITUATED** *in the heart of the business centre of Montreal, and is contiguous to the General Post Office and other important public buildings.*

It is Handsomely Decorated, Luxuriously Furnished, Lighted by Electric Light, and Fitted with a Passenger Elevator.

The Building, which has recently been extended, contains 350 rooms, has an elegant new Parlor, and the Dining Room has been recently enlarged and renovated, making it one of the finest in Canada.

THE HOTEL IS MANAGED BY MR. SAMUEL MONTGOMERY, UNDER THE PERSONAL SUPERVISION OF MR. HENRY HOGAN.

Strachan's
Gilt Edge Soap
IS THE BEST.

STRACHAN'S
GILT-EDGE SOAP

Takes First Place Wherever used.

9 781014 835444